22 FEB 2002

613.2

TIREE HIGH SCHOOL
LIBRARY

WISE h GUIDES

EATING

Anita Naik

Illustrated by James Tyrrell
Consultant: Susie Orbach
author of *Fat is a Feminist Issue*

D0301087

34115 00482261 1

ted

Text copyright 1999 © Anita Naik
Illustrations copyright 1999 © James Tyrrell
Published by Hodder Children's Books 1999

Design by Fiona Webb

The rights of Anita Naik and James Tyrrell to be identified as the author
and illustrator of the Work have been asserted by them in
accordance with the Copyright, Designs and Patents Act 1988.

10 9 8 7 6 5 4 3

ISBN: 0 340 74411 1

All rights reserved. No part of this publication may be reproduced,
stored in a retrieval system, or transmitted, in any form or by any
means, without the prior written permission of the publisher, nor be
otherwise circulated in any form of binding or cover other than that in
which it is published and without a similar condition being imposed on
the subsequent purchaser.

The information in this book has been thoroughly researched
and checked for accuracy. Neither the author nor the publisher
can accept any responsibility for any loss, injury or damage
incurred as a result of using this book.

Printed by The Guernsey Press Co. Ltd, Guernsey, C.I.

Hodder Children's Books
a division of Hodder Headline Limited
338 Euston Road
London NW1 3BH

Contents

Other essential

BULLYING
Michele Elliott

DIVORCE AND SEPARATION
Matthew Whyman

DRUGS
Anita Naik

PERIODS
Charlotte Owen

SELF-ESTEEM
Anita Naik

SEX
Anita Naik

See pages 131–134 for more details.

Introduction

Looking and feeling good isn't about what size clothes you wear, what you weigh or what you eat. It's about having a positive view of yourself and being kind to yourself, no matter what you eat or don't eat.

Let's face it, we all have ugly days. Days when our stomachs look too big, our faces look too weird and we believe we're the ugliest creature on earth. However, bad days aside, everyone should also have great days when they feel gorgeous and good about themselves.

If you never have days like this, it's time to take a long hard (and more honest) look at your self image. Eating, and not eating, should not control the way you feel about your life and body. If it does it's time to reassess the way you think. And that's where this book comes in.

If you want to know how to cope with the perils of eating, this book will show you why diets are a big no-no, how you can eat the things you love and stay healthy, and what to do if you really, really hate your body.

So don't despair, you can start to change the way you feel about yourself today. All you have to do is turn the page ...

Anita

● QUIZ ●

HOW DO YOU FEEL ABOUT YOUR BODY?

1 You're in the changing rooms of a store,
   trying on a top. It doesn't look too great.
   What do you do?
   a) Quickly rip it off before someone sees you.
      You always look fat and lumpy in everything
      you wear.
   b) Sneak a look around to see if anyone else
      looks worse than you do.
   c) Decide the top doesn't suit you and go back
      into the shop to find something that does.

2 Every morning when you look in the mirror,
   what do you think?
   a) You never look in mirrors if you can help it.
   b) I wish I were thinner/fatter/taller/smaller.
   c) Why do I always look terrible in the mornings?

3 Would you feel uncomfortable going round
   with a friend who was either very slim, or
   very overweight?
   a) Yes, you'd be afraid other people would
      compare you to them.
   b) No – you don't choose your friends by the
      way they look.
   c) Yes, but you would never let on because you
      would never hurt their feelings.

4 **What kind of person do you consider to be beautiful?**

   a) All different kinds of people.

   b) Usually a famous actress or model.

   c) Anyone but yourself.

5 **If you could change one thing about yourself, what would it be?**

   a) A personality trait

   b) A body part

   c) The whole package

6 **How do you feel about wearing a swimsuit on the beach?**

   a) Horrified, so you cover up with a T-shirt.

   b) Worried, but you know lots of people feel embarrassed about wearing one.

   c) You'd never wear one.

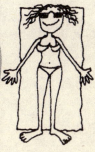   

7 **You catch sight of your reflection in a shop window. What are you likely to do?**
   a) Take a closer look to make sure your hair looks okay, and your stomach's not sticking out.
   b) Look away quickly and try to erase what you've seen from your mind.
   c) Look at yourself critically and feel bad the rest of the afternoon.

8 **Do you ever feel your life would be perfect if ...**
   a) You were thinner/fatter.
   b) You had more freedom.
   c) You were someone else.

9 **You think you're fat but people tell you ...**
   a) You're average.
   b) You're obsessed with your weight.
   c) You should eat more.

10 **How do you feel when you eat chocolate and crisps?**
   a) Horribly guilty and so you skip dinner.
   b) Fine
   c) Depressed so you eat more.

SCORES

1	a10	b5	c0
2	a5	b10	c0
3	a10	b0	c5
4	a0	b5	c10
5	a0	b5	c10
6	a5	b0	c10
7	a0	b10	c5
8	a10	b0	c5
9	a0	b5	c10
10	a5	b0	c10

RESULTS

0 – 30 The body beautiful

Congratulations. You have a healthy view of both your body and your life. You're happy the way you are and aren't seeking perfection. Maybe you don't need to read this book! Then again, it won't hurt to polish up your knowledge on looking and feeling healthy.

35 – 65 The body not-so-bad

Okay, so you don't totally hate your body, but you could do with learning to be more comfortable with the way you look. This book can help you to learn to be confident about your body and show you how not to let what you eat control your life.

70–100 The body you hate

Could you be harder on yourself? I can guarantee you that no-one sees your body the way you currently see it. But don't despair, help is at hand, if you read on.

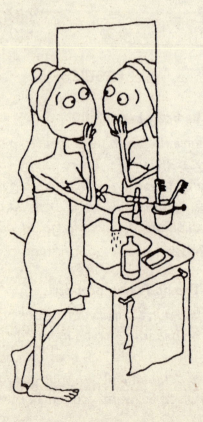

CHAPTER ONE

The problem with eating

Remember when you loved the sight of your body? How old were you? Five, eight, ten? Whatever age you were, I bet you didn't mind the whole world seeing you in a bathing suit and I'm sure you didn't care what food you ate. Think about yourself now. Do you still feel like this, or do you, like thousands of other people, have a case of bad-body-image?

If you're reading this book, then we'll take it that body image and eating (whether you're big, small, short or tall) are an issue for you. If this is the case then it's likely you want to change your body, to get thinner/ bigger/taller/shorter. If this is right, it's also likely you've got a pretty good image of what your 'perfect' body would look like.

If you're a girl, is it being 5' 10", with a 34 C chest? Or is it a size 10 with a flat chest? Maybe it's a combination of the above, or something completely different. Or perhaps, like a lot of the TV shows, you believe the perfect body entails long blonde hair, big breasts and a slim body.

And what about an attractive man? What does he look like? Tall and muscular with a killer six pack? Or maybe you consider someone thin with androgynous features more fashionable. Or perhaps the hourglass figure is what you're after!

"I am big and fat. 'Pleasantly plump' says my gran, but I'm fat and tall and that's why no-one ever asks me out. I don't blame them. I don't want to go out with someone who looks like me."

Karen (13)

"I'd love to be a model, but when I told my friends they all laughed and said because of my big chest the only model I could be was a Page Three girl. I hate my chest. I do everything I can think of to make it look smaller, like dieting and baggy jumpers, but nothing works."

Shona, 14

"I'm so skinny that when I hold my breath you can see my ribs – it's disgusting. If I was taller I could probably be a model, instead I'm called pancake girl at school. Flat and ugly – that's me."

Susie, 13

Of course as you can see, feeling that you are not the 'right' weight is one of the most common ways of not fitting into an idea of being 'perfect'. This is why what you eat, whether you want to put weight on, take it off or transfer it around your body, can become such a major issue.

THE RISE AND FALL OF THE IDEAL BODY

In a hundred years what do you think will be the shape of the 'ideal body'? Will technology and space travel have advanced so far that today's sci-fi images of aliens with elongated legs and big eyes will influence the supermodels of the 21st century? Far-fetched maybe, but the popular notion of an attractive body has changed constantly throughout history and even today never stays the same.

A hundred years ago the 'perfect vision of beauty' was a woman with a healthy and robust body, small hands, and small feet (which naturally rules out today's 6' supermodels). This idea of beauty meant a good supply of body weight was an essential part of being attractive. Waists were artificially sucked in with corsets, to create a look of ample breasts, big hips and bottoms. However, the price of being fashionable was high, and many women were hospitalised for fainting and cracked ribs, all caused by the tightness of the corsets.

1920s

By the 1920s this image had changed considerably; plump was out and thin was in. According to the fashions of the day, girls wore their skirts at knee length. Corsets were no longer used and flat chests were 'in'. Girls with bigger breasts bound them down to look fashionable, and the idea of dieting started to become popular.

1940s/50s

A mere twenty years later, breasts were back in a big way, but to this long legs were the added essential. Actresses like Betty Grable and Rita Hayworth and later Marilyn Monroe, were considered to be the perfect beauties. The emphasis was on bodies that resembled the classic voluptuous, hourglass figure. Weight was in again, but this time it had to be distributed in certain areas only.

1960s

By the time the so-called sexual revolution hit the 1960s, the fashionable female figure had changed again. This time the thinnest views of the female form ever to be considered were introduced via models such as Twiggy and Jean Shrimpton. Skinny was in, and if you were average or bigger than average you were in trouble.

1970s/80s

In the 70s, big was for a short time considered beautiful, with earth mother types with big bodies and breasts being literally in *Vogue*. However, by the 1980s a new phenomenon hit the streets – the supermodel. Suddenly athleticism was in and the stronger, taller and leaner you looked the more society was likely to consider you beautiful.

1990s

Again, the backlash arrived and the 90s saw the arrival of the complete opposite – the waifs – tiny, minuscule girls, who gave out the message that to be not just slim but thin was to be beautiful.

As you can see, if you were someone who had tried to keep up with fashion over a hundred year period you would have spent most of the time pumping up your breasts and weight, only to have to deflate them all over again. It's little wonder many of us feel confused and discouraged about our bodies!

When it comes to what you should look like, who's right and who's wrong? Well, no-one, because if the truth be told, beauty really is in the eye of the beholder. Different looks do it for different people and so the only thing that's really important is how you feel about yourself.

TOO FAT, TOO THIN

Of course, if you do feel negative about your body, you're not alone. Talk to any of the girls or boys you know, your mum, your sister, your friends, your relatives and the chances are, they are as unhappy with their weight as the following people:

"I always feel such a failure about being fat. It's like I am this disgusting person who can't control myself."

Lisa, 14, weighs 11 stone

"The worst part of being fat is not being able to wear trendy clothes. I can't shop in *Miss Selfridge* and *Top Shop* because I'd just never fit into those things. I have to just wear baggy sweatshirts and trousers."

Becca, 14

"I hate my body. I'm short and puny and get called names like Bony, and Skeleton by my so-called friends. I once asked this girl out and she laughed in my face saying, 'Why would I go out with a skinny geek like you?'"

Tom, 11

"Everyone says I'm lucky to be so thin, but the truth is no boys fancy me. They go for the girls who are curvy and have a shape. No matter what I eat, my bones still stick out and I look like a freak."

Samantha, 13

"I want to look like those guys in the adverts, with muscles and height. Instead I look like one of those guys people always pick on in comedy films. You know the little guy with the glasses."

Jack, 12

"Girls make out it's easier to be fat if you're boy but it's not. When I walk down the school corridors, I hear people saying things like here comes the fat boy, hide your sweets."

Paul, 11

"I get depressed when I look in the mirror. I'm like an ironing board, straight up and straight down. Once I kissed this boy and he said he couldn't go out with me because it would be like dating a boy."

Jill, 13

THE PRESSURE TO BE "THIN"

So where does the pressure to be thin come from? The fact is, eating should be one of the great pleasures in life and yet, because of the messages we all receive about food and weight, many of us find it a battleground.

Contrary to what you might believe, humans are not programmed to diet or to fear weight gain. We learn those beliefs from the messages around us. Messages we pick up from our peer group, the media, our mothers, advertising and our families. Messages that tell us we'd be happier/more successful, and much sexier, if only we were thinner. In most cases we are bombarded for so long with this idea, that we eventually start to believe it and enter a world where food and being fat are the reasons why we are unhappy with our lives.

This is why it's important to move your focus away from what others tell you about your body. Instead you need to learn to look at what is most healthy for you – both physically and emotionally.

The mother-daughter connection

"My mum says I'm too fat and stops me from eating the things I want. I hate it and just eat those things when she's not around."

Liz, 12

"We eat different meals to my brothers. They get chips and burgers, we get cottage cheese and salad."

Hannah, 13

"When I was 8 years old my mum told me I was fat and needed to on a diet, otherwise no boy would like me. From then on we have dieted together."

Jilly, 13

" I have to go to *Weight Watchers*™ every week. I really hate it. I am the only kid there, everyone else is my mother's age. I find it embarrassing and shaming."

Donna, 15

More and more studies show that there is a strong connection between mothers and daughters when it comes to attitudes about weight. This is not to say that these attitudes are an hereditary trait, but more that they are something we learn from our mothers.

Take 13-year-old Tara, who has been worried about her weight since she was nine years old. For the last two years she has been dieting and recently she has started attending a slimming class with her mum. However, two months ago her doctor told her she was not overweight.

"I know I'm not really fat, I'm just fat. My doctor told my mum I was at a healthy weight but I want to be thinner. I want to lose weight so I can look good and not be miserable. My mum understands this because she used to be fat. Now she is quite thin but says that weight was the cause of all her teenage problems. She says the reason why she never got dates was because she was fat and boys don't like fat girls.

She's not being mean, she just doesn't want me to go
through what she went through. She hasn't pushed me into
dieting, in fact she is the only person who has helped me.
We usually diet together to support each other and try to
eat the same foods. It's not bad really because some of my
friends' mums won't let them diet and they have to lie about
it. At least I don't have to do that, we're really open in our
house about weight."

Tara, like many girls, believes her mum is helping her
to deal with her eating fears, and her mum, like many
mothers, believes she is helping her daughter.
However, the problem is that the mother-daughter
connection is exactly how negative eating patterns are
passed on from generation to generation.

If you think there may be a connection between your
mother, your attitude to food and your feelings about
eating, consider if your mum does any of the
following:

- eats different meals to the rest of the family
- comments on how much you eat and tries to stop
  you from eating more
- says how much happier you'd be if you controlled
  your weight
- suggests clothes look better when you're thin
- claims she would be happier if she were thin
- says mean things about her own body
- weighs herself every day
- avoids looking in mirrors
- denies herself foods she likes because they are 'bad'
  for her

These are just some of the ways you may find yourself being influenced by your mum. The problem is, what do you do if you have a mother who is unhappy about her weight, obsessed with dieting and worried about you becoming fat? How can you get her to give you some space, so you can discover some positive feelings about your body?

HOW TO TALK TO YOUR MOTHER ABOUT WEIGHT

- Tell her studies show that restricting foods, imposing control over eating and setting up eating rules only give a person an unhealthy attitude to food.
- Explain exactly how what she says about your weight makes you feel about yourself. Often mothers don't realise their words are both hurtful and damaging.
- Suggest you concentrate on eating healthily instead of dieting and explain this is because you don't want to grow up having an unhealthy attitude to food (see chapters 5 and 6).

- Remember, it may be extremely difficult for your mother to feel positive about your weight if she hates her own body. Encourage her to start thinking about her reasons for dieting.
- Question her when she says mean things about how she looks and encourage her to find good things to say about herself.
- Sit down together and try and come up with positive female role models who don't have size 10 bodies.

Other family influences

While mothers are usually the main source for the information we get about food and our body images, we're also influenced by other family members.

FATHERS

"My dad is always commenting on what I eat. If he wants me to stop eating sweets, he says stuff like, 'You're so big, whatever happened to my little girl?'. He thinks I'm ugly and wants me to be prettier. It's a horrible feeling to know he thinks that."

Claire, 11

Whether it's insensitivity or conscious behaviour, lots of fathers say negative things like this when their daughters hit adolescence. If you have a father who is making you feel bad about your body, try pointing out that:

- His views are making you feel bad about yourself.
- You need him to be positive, not negative, about the way you are.

Also ask yourself if what you think he means is what he *really* means. When we're sensitive about our bodies, it's easy to take other people's comments the wrong way.

SIBLINGS

> "My brother calls me fatso and it makes me feel really bad. I ask him to stop all the time but he won't."
>
> Chloe, 13

> "My sister is tiny and very slim. Next to her I look like an elephant. It doesn't help that my parents call her the pretty one, and me the clever one."
>
> Tanya, 12

Siblings can be horrible, simply because they know they are related to you and can get away with it. If you have a sibling who teases you about the way you look, or your parents treat you and your siblings differently, here's what you can do.

- Ask your parents to treat you both equally. They may not know that they are hurting your feelings.
- Enlist your parents' help in stopping sibling teasing.
- Explain to your family how the teasing makes you feel .

Peer pressure

> "Sometimes I get really depressed because my friends are always going on about being fat. The thing is they're thinner than me, so I must be really fat and that means they're too scared to tell me."
>
> Helen, 13

"At lunch we all make a big thing of eating only half our sandwiches. Sometimes I want to eat more, but I don't want everyone to think I'm being a fat pig."

Paula, 13

"I don't really want to diet but all the girls I know do. It's like if you're a girl you have to diet or else everyone thinks you're mad."

Sophie, 12

The pressure from friends to diet and focus on our weight is one of the biggest influences making us become victims of the bad body image. After all, sitting down to lunch every day with a bunch of teenagers who are being competitive about what they do and don't eat is no fun. No-one likes to feel they're the odd one out and it can be hard to make an independent stand by changing the subject. But when it comes to dieting and feeling good about yourself, you have to consider that your body is yours and yours alone. Is it really worth setting yourself on a path to misery just so you won't feel left out?

HOW TO TALK TO YOUR FRIENDS ABOUT WEIGHT

- Stand up for what you believe in. If your friends start talking about dieting, start talking about how diets are unhealthy (see chapter 4).
- Challenge the messages you hear from your friends about weight and attractiveness. Are all happy people really thin? Does everyone have to be a size 10? Will skipping lunch/breakfast really help you lose weight?
- Would you fancy a boy if he didn't have a 'perfect' body? If you would, what makes you think boys don't fancy girls with 'imperfect' bodies?
- Think about some good role models who you and your friends admire for reasons other than looks – for instance, women you admire for their intelligence, humour or their work.

Whatever you do, stick to what you want to eat, don't let your friends convince you certain foods are 'bad' for you.

The media

"Famous people are always thin."

Wendy, 12

"Magazines and adverts are to blame for how I feel. They are always full of skinny models."

Fiona, 12

"Why aren't there more fat people on TV and in magazines? The models are always so thin."

Sara, 13

Yes, the media is full of images of thin women and yes, female models are always skinny. And the reason why they're always skinny is to make the clothes they wear look more attractive, so that more people will buy them (because we've been brainwashed into believing that clothes look better on thin women!). Therefore, having skinny models adorn the fashion pages of magazines is not about beauty but money. However, we're so used to seeing fashion and beauty depicted with thin models, we forget why it's happening and associate beauty with being thin.

While it's easy to blame the media for our feelings about weight, we all have to learn to take responsibility for ourselves. This means if we buy a fashion magazine, we know we are going to be bombarded with pictures of thin women, which may or may not make us feel bad.

If you don't want to look at these women, you don't have to buy the magazine. And while this doesn't solve the problem of the media's influence on our body images, it is a start in reclaiming control of how you feel about yourself.

HOW TO STAND UP TO THE MEDIA

- Make a choice about what you look at and take responsibility for it.
- If you're going to look at fashion magazines, be aware of how you are viewing the models and how you are feeling about yourself.
- If you want to see more realistic images of women, look at the women around you.

- Consider all the many and varied women in the public eye. Not all are thin. Many of the most successful women in politics, journalism, newscasting, comedy and film do not fulfil the classic idea of beauty.
- Fashion is about looking a certain way at a certain time. You are always free to disagree with it and look the way you want.

CHAPTER TWO

Puberty, food and fat

"Love yourself."
"Feel good inside and you'll feel good out."
"It's personality that counts."
"What you look like doesn't matter."

We've all heard the above and thought deep down, yes that's true, but let's face it, it often doesn't *feel* true. The fact is, it's hard to feel good about yourself and your body when your body keeps changing in unexpected ways. At puberty, the body enters a rapid period of growth that you can do little about, and it can make you feel as if you're trapped in someone else's body.

"I hate my body now. I used to look small and I liked that; now I have stretch marks on my back, and the tops of my legs, and I'm taller then everyone in my class. I'm skinny and long on the outside but inside I feel like someone else."

Zena, 13

"I don't fit into any of my old clothes any more. Since I got my periods, my body just sticks out everywhere. My bottom sticks out, my chest sticks out, my tummy sticks out. I'm a blob."

Laura, 14

"I waited for ages for my periods to start but if I'd known it meant my body would get fat, I wouldn't have wanted them to start. I hate the way I look and feel. I hate puberty."

Anya, 13

Like the girls quoted above, it's easy to put the blame for feeling and looking bad on puberty. However, understanding why your body changes and why you put on weight at this time can help you to become more comfortable with your body and how you look.

WHAT IS PUBERTY?

Puberty is the term given for the bodily changes which transform you from a child into an adult. It's a time when many people begin to feel weird about their bodies because they are changing shape and naturally developing. For girls these body changes include the start of your periods, an increase in height, the growth of your sex organs, the appearance of pubic hair, the development of your breasts, the activation of your body's sweat glands and an increase in weight.

For boys these changes include the production of sperm, an increase in height, the growth of your sex organs, the appearance of body hair, and weight gain.

What happens to your body at puberty?

While puberty happens to everyone, it rarely happens at the same time. Many girls start puberty around the age of 10, but many others will start earlier or later, so some girls will start to gain curves, height and weight well before their friends. Boys tend to start puberty on average a couple of years later than girls, but again this varies. Each person has their own personal clock, which regulates when their body will change and how.

What girls can expect between the ages of 9 – 14 years

- Breasts will start to develop. This will happen at roughly 10 – 12 years. Development can take up to six years.
- A growth spurt will begin around the age of 10 and usually speeds up between 11 and 12.
- As soon as your growth spurt starts, your body's weight and height increase.
- Periods begin (usually 1–2 years after your breasts begin to grow).
- Hip bones grow wider in girls and fat begins to deposit under the skin to give you the characteristic female body shape.

What boys can expect between the ages of 11 – 16 years

While the majority of boys start puberty around the age of 11 or 12, many boys find they start earlier or later.

- Testicles start to grow and the bag of skin that contains them (the scrotum) will darken and hang lower. This will happen before the age of 14.
- A growth spurt usually begins around the age of 11 and happens the quickest between 12 and 14.
- At this stage your body's weight and height will increase rapidly.
- At around the age of 13, body hair will start to grow, pubic hair will appear, as will underarm hair.
- Facial hair begins to grow.
- Shoulders grow wider, limbs grow longer.
- The voice breaks, in other words becomes deeper.

How and why your body changes

All these changes are completely normal and cause a natural weight gain. As scary as this might sound, puberty is a spectacular event which proves your body is well on its way to adulthood.

The changes are triggered off by chemicals in our bodies called hormones which are released from small organs called endocrine glands. Once they have been released, they travel around your body, via the bloodstream, to different organs, and when they arrive at a particular place, such as your bones, they cause the area to change and grow.

The most important female sex hormone is oestrogen, and this is produced by the ovaries. It is this hormone which causes the development of the breasts, the start of your periods and the laying down of fat around your body.

The most important male hormone is testosterone, which is responsible for the growth of limbs and the male sex organs.

Why girls need body fat at puberty

"Why do we need more fat when we get older? Why don't our bodies stay the same?"

Tina, 11

Prior to puberty, a girl's body only carries 12% of body fat because you're smaller and not in need of so much energy. But at puberty this changes and with a surge of hormone production, body fat levels rise to about 18% to 28% to support the body's bones and muscles as they grow to adult size.

All in all 20–26% of an adult woman's weight consists of fat (15–20% for a man) and if you want to know where this fat is distributed, take a look at any woman's body. It's usually concentrated on her thighs, bottom, breasts, and hips, places where it's most needed to keep the female body fertile and healthy.

Why you need fat for your fertility

"What have periods got to do with putting on weight?"
Jill, 11

Fat deposits in the body are essential because if you don't have enough body fat, then not only will your periods stop, but you'll be less fertile (i.e. less able to have a baby) and more at risk in later life from being hunched over and having brittle bones – osteoporosis. This is because body fat is needed to keep up the production of the female hormone oestrogen, and bones need oestrogen to stay healthy.

How periods affect your weight

"I get even more worried about my weight around my periods because I feel hungry all the time and have to eat chocolate."

Susie, 14

Many women associate weight gain with menstruating because they find their weight fluctuates throughout their menstrual cycle. However, this has more to do with retaining water than fat. In fact, studies show some women can retain 4 to 6 lbs of water before each period. This results in feeling bloated in the abdomen and tenderness in the breast area. The body retains this water to make sure cells are hydrated throughout menstruation. Once your period starts, the water will be lost naturally with the rest of your period. Other women worry about their weight around their periods because they find they not only crave sweet things, but also feel hungry all the time. This kind of hunger occurs because during the last 10 days of a cycle, the body often needs more calories for energy. Again you don't need to worry about this as the need for extra food is completely natural.

Weight fluctuates throughout menstrual cycle. Water retention, feeling bloated.

Breasts and weight gain

"Why is it that some skinny girls have big breasts and some fat girls have small breasts?"

Jenni, 11

The first sign of puberty for most girls are growing breasts. When these first start to develop they are known as breast buds and many girls find these buds tender and often uneven in size. This is quite normal and eventually they will become more even. Breasts take quite a long time to reach the size they are going to be, so what you start out with may not necessarily be what you end up with.

Like weight, many women aren't happy about their breast size, feeling they'd rather be smaller or larger. Again, though breast size is partially affected by weight, it is largely determined by hereditary factors passed down from your parents.

Why boys need fat

"Do boys need body fat too?"

Tom, 13

Though adult men naturally have less body fat than women (because men don't need fat to generate oestrogen and periods), boys, like girls, need body fat too. Body fat is the fuel your body uses to make the body grow so if you don't eat enough, your body has nothing to grow on. What's more, because you have more muscle mass than women, you need more energy (from fat and food) to keep your body fit and healthy.

FOOD, FAT AND YOU

"I saw a programme on TV where this women had fat taken out of her bottom. It came out all orange and disgusting looking. It made me feel sick to think of all that stuff lying in my body."

Mel, 14

Most people think fat is bad because these days it's drummed into us that we should avoid it. It's ridiculous really, because fat is a substance that is essential to the human body. We all need it to maintain and sustain our lives.

Body fat is needed to coat our bodies' cells, cushion our organs from damage, stop us from feeling the cold, and most importantly, supply our bodies with the energy and fuel they need to do everyday things from walking to talking.

The only problem with fat is, our bodies love to store it. Storing food as fat has been part of the human survival process for thousands of years. It was our bodies' way of surviving times of famine, by having a source of energy to look for food when it was scarce without starving. Of course, these days we're not so active and

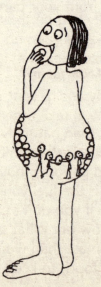

The only problem with fat is our bodies love to store it.

a trip down to your local supermarket isn't as calorie burning as having to hunt and gather food. This is why excess body fat doesn't get burnt up and why so many people who aren't active are at risk from carrying more weight than they need.

Why we need to eat

Food is energy, also known as calories. Calories are a unit of measurement – a way of calculating how much energy a certain piece of food has. If you don't eat you'll have no fuel in your body to do the things you want to do. What's more, if you skip meals, fast or crash diet, you will be doing a great disservice to your body because your metabolism will shut down. This means the rate at which you expel energy will slow down (think of an engine working at half its capacity). The body will then start taking energy from other places.

Your body will cling on to any remaining fat, and instead you'll end up losing lean muscle mass (which is bad news because it's muscle that actually burns up fat). Overall, this means that the second you start eating properly again, your metabolism will be confused and will take time to re-adjust.

What is metabolism?

Metabolism is the rate at which your body burns energy (fat/calories). Your metabolic rate varies throughout your life – it will naturally work faster at puberty and slow down around middle age. But, unlike other genetic factors, we can affect our metabolic rate. Turn it up through exercise and you will lose more fat; turn it down and you will hold on to fat.

Our metabolism also changes on a daily basis. Before you wake up in the morning it is at its slowest, but as the day proceeds it increases, peaking at around lunchtime. Therefore if you want to boost your metabolic rate, exercise and eat soon after waking up and you will burn calories for longer.

However, the most important way of boosting your metabolism is to actually eat and not skip meals. This is because when the body receives calories through food it responds by upping the metabolic rate and burning more calories. Skip meals and it has nothing to work on and will slow down.

WHAT IS A HEALTHY WEIGHT?

 "One minute I hear being fat is bad for you, the next I hear that being skinny is bad for you. I looked my weight up on two charts. One said I was fine, the other said I was overweight. It's all so confusing."

Janine, 14

A healthy weight is not:

- Being at a weight you have to deny yourself food to stay at.
- What a height/weight chart says (see below).
- What other people term 'normal'.
- Falling into the right % in a body fat % test.
- Being at a weight that makes you feel ill and tired all the time.

The fact is, we are all biologically unique, and this means we all have a different weight that is right for us. Take a look at the following body shapes to see how there's no such thing as 'normal'.

ENDOMORPH   MESOMORPH   ECTOMORPH

Endomorph

People who are this shape tend to be apple shaped. Weight is usually placed around the stomach area. Their torsos are long, and legs slightly shorter. Breasts tend to be slightly bigger than average and they have round faces. Their bone structure is light and they tend to be short to average in height. Endomorphs gain weight more easily than the other body types.

Mesomorph

People who are mesomorphs are more pear shaped. Their hips are larger than their shoulders and their legs are the same size as their torsos. Weight is collected around the hips, thighs and bottom. They mostly have square or oval faces and are of average or above average height.

Ectomorph

Ectomorphs are tall and slim, with strong bone structures. They have long legs and oval faces. They don't gain weight easily and any weight they do gain is distributed evenly across their body.

Weight charts

Hands up if you've ever used a weight chart? The ones where you find your height, link it up to the weight you're currently at, and then find out if you are underweight, normal, overweight, or obese. How about those mechanisms that measure the percentage of your body fat, or the equations that tell you how much you should weigh? Have you tried them and felt crushed at the result?

If you have, you're not alone. These methods are very generalised and always compare you to a norm that may not apply. If you don't believe me, consider this: weight charts are currently going through their *eighth* revision on weight recommendations! Look closely at these charts and you'll see the margins between being normal and overweight are very slim. Look once more and you'll see they make little or no reference to build, hereditary factors or fitness.

So how do you select you goal weight if weight charts are too vague? Well, experts now agree that people should base their weight on how they feel, not on a chart. This is based on the principle that most of us (eating disorders aside) have a pretty good idea of what weight we feel comfortable and healthy at, and what weight we don't. This may not conform perfectly to a chart or a percentage figure but it's ultimately something we can sustain and be happy with.

If you're unsure about your weight, consider these questions.

1 Does your body weight restrict you from doing what you want in any way?
2 Do you find it hard to move your body easily?
3 When you run for a bus does your heart feel as if it's going to burst?

Three 'yes's' and you're probably not at your healthy weight and need to start eating healthily and incorporating exercise into your life (see chapters 6 and 8). Three 'no's' and you're probably OK!

Why 99% of us won't look like supermodels

"I want to be a model but I'm only 5' 4". It's so unfair – I want to be tall and skinny, not short and fat."

Anne, 14

Like it or not, the way you look has a lot to do with your genes – a kind of growth map you are born with.

Basically, all the information our bodies need for our physical and emotional growth are carried in something called chromosomes. Each chromosome consists of two chains of DNA, made up of thousands of pairs of genes, which in turn have been inherited from our parents.

It's these genes which play a vital role in determining what shape we will be. This means how big or small our hips, breasts or chests are, or how tall we get have all been determined before we are born.

This means if you have large hips and bottoms and a small bust, it's likely your mother and/or grandmother had this too and so will your children. Therefore, no amount of exercise and dieting will give you a large bust, small hips and a non-existent bottom.

However, you cannot blame genes for everything. Though genetics permit some of us to get fat, or become obese, they don't cause it. Eating healthily and exercising to make the best of what you were born with is still your choice.

CHAPTER THREE

Food and feelings

Question: Why do we eat?
Answer: Because we're hungry.

At least that's what we're supposed to do: eat when we're hungry and stop eating when we're full. The trouble is, eating is not always about being hungry. Sometimes it's about feeling sad or depressed. Other times it's about rebelling or trying to be a 'good' girl or boy for the people you're with.

When we're little kids, before we're influenced by our friends, parents and society's eating rules, our body knows how to respond to eating without any problem. It lets us know when to eat, how much to eat and when to stop eating. This naturally means we don't have to worry about our weight because we only eat what we need and then run around and work it all off, until we need to eat again.

Unfortunately, though, when you still live at home, you don't have the ability to make decisions about when to eat. This is when you stop listening to your hunger signals and instead of choosing to eat when you're hungry, you eat when your parents/school/society says.

As you get older you also start to lose track of exactly why you're eating, because food starts to take on meanings that have little to do with hunger. For instance, it becomes about what you can and can't eat and how you should eat and you acquire social habits that have very little to do with your own instinctive eating habits. It's at this point that eating can start to take on negative meanings to do with weight and fatness, instead of being something you enjoy doing.

HOW YOU CAN LOSE TRACK OF WHY YOU EAT

Fear of becoming fat

"I don't eat very much even when I'm hungry because I don't want to be fat. My 17-year-old sister is fat and it's horrible. I love her but I feel ashamed when I look at her. My mum is always telling her she'd be pretty if she lost weight, and people are always calling her names on the street, but she never listens. In fact all she does is eat more."

Dee, 13

The associations we make about becoming or being fat can often lead us to restrict the way we eat. In Dee's case, her sister's situation has given her strong messages about how society treats people who don't look a certain way. Dee won't eat because she doesn't want to become like her sister and be ridiculed for being overweight. However, pushing your hunger away and ignoring it is as much of a problem as eating when you're not really hungry.

Parents who control what you eat

"My mother gets really annoyed with me and says I am a compulsive eater just because I get hungry all the time. She won't let me eat between meals and will never let me have seconds, so I often have to sneak around and take food when she's not looking."

Ellie, 13

"My parents are always nagging me to eat up and not waste food. If I say I'm not hungry, or refuse to eat something my mum freaks and accuses me of being anorexic. Sometimes I wish I was because then that would really make her feel bad."

Tina, 15

Studies show that when parents leave their kids alone to make their own choices about eating, children adjust their food intake accordingly and consume the right amount of food their bodies need. However, this is easier said than done and food can be a big issue in families because parents worry that their kids aren't eating enough or are eating too much. The reasons for this may be social (because parents know it's their job to make sure you eat properly) or personal (they may have food issues themselves).

Therefore, if you have parents who make you eat food when you're not hungry, it's up to you to reassure them that you are being sensible and not skipping meals or on some faddy diet. If, on the other hand, your parents are trying to control your eating and make you eat less, you need to talk to them about how their actions make you feel. After all, research shows that people who are denied food when they want to eat often crave food all the more, and usually end up secretly eating more.

Friends who watch what they eat

"Whenever I eat chocolate or crisps in front of my
friends they say, 'You should be careful you'll get fat'.
It makes me worry because none of them ever eat the
wrong things."

Lee, 13

"My friend says if you want to control your weight you
need to skip meals. She never eats her lunch and makes
a big thing about throwing it away everyday. I feel bad
because I always eat mine. I have no willpower like her."

Maria, 13

Sometimes a friend can be your worst enemy, especially when it comes to eating. Research shows many girls learn 'rules' about eating from their friends and peer groups.

It can be hard to stand up to friends about what you eat and why, especially when their comments make you feel like you're being 'greedy', or when their behaviour makes you feel you're the one doing something wrong. Many girls and women are given the message that it's okay to be competitive about food. They may act like martyrs for not eating and yet feel secretly happy that you're eating more than them. Try not to give in to that, because the fact is, everyone is made differently. We all need to eat different amounts at different times. If you are hungry and want to eat, that's your decision. Don't let yourself be pulled into someone else's bad eating habits.

EATING FOR REASONS OTHER THAN HUNGER

1 Depression - eating to avoid facing your problems

"Last month my boyfriend broke up with me and he started seeing my best friend. I feel really depressed about it but I don't want to lose face so I make out it doesn't bother me. To feel better I've started eating and drinking a lot – it helps a bit because it stops me thinking about what's happened."

Lorraine, 15

Feeling depressed is a tough one. However, 'depressed' is sometimes one of those words we use as a blanket term that doesn't really get to the bottom of how we're really feeling. If you're someone who feels depressed, you need to try to work out exactly what you're feeling and why. What are you upset about? Are you angry? Sad? Frustrated?

What's making you feel bad? Do you feel no-one understands you? If so, why?

If you can't talk about how you feel then try writing it down. Repressing your feelings won't make them go away.

2 Self loathing - eating because you hate yourself

"I hate myself. If you really knew me you would too. I'm fat, I'm ugly and I know no-one likes me. The only time I feel okay is when I eat."

Sian, 14

We all have inner conversations about how we feel about ourselves. For people with low self esteem, these conversations focus around how 'bad' we are and how we don't match up to others. If you also feel you have a weight problem, this probably only adds to your fears about yourself. Again, the way out of this kind of self loathing is to learn how to express how you feel to someone you trust. You *can* conquer low self esteem! (See chapter 7.)

3 Guilt — eating because you feel you shouldn't

"I feel bad about being fat so I eat something I know is bad for me, but once I've eaten something bad I feel guilty about it and then feel even worse. This means I then eat some more to feel better. It's horrible. I feel trapped."

Toni, 14

Feeling guilty about eating has little to do with food and a lot to do with the beliefs you hold about what you should and shouldn't allow yourself to eat. The fact is there are no good and bad foods. If you choose to classify food as good and bad you are bound to sabotage yourself because as soon as you eat the 'bad' food, you will automatically feel guilty and feel you have done something 'wrong'. It's human to crave the things we forbid ourselves, so make your life easy and think of food as food, and nothing else (see chapter 6 for more information on Healthy Eating).

4 Avoidance – eating to take yourself out of the game

> "I'm fat already so no-one's ever going to want to go out with me. I know this is true because boys just don't want to talk to me, they only make fun of me. I may as well just get really fat - no-one would care."
>
> Laurie, 13

Sometimes people eat because they feel uncomfortable about new feelings they are experiencing. If these feelings are painful or difficult to comprehend, it can be easier to choose to become something you know is not socially acceptable. But such avoidance tactics eventually bring you right back round to where you began. You are better off facing your feelings, no matter how difficult they may be.

5 Trauma – eating to avoid feeling

> "Ever since my dad died my weight has gone up and up. I keep pretending it doesn't matter and I don't know how it's happening but I do. Every time I think about my dad I feel sad, and then I eat because it helps me to forget and for a while I feel better."
>
> Sarah, 16

> "When I get upset I reach for food - it makes me feel better. The problem is I get upset all the time these days, so I can't stop eating."
>
> Susie, 14

Lots of people use food as a way to cushion their pain and avoid something traumatic in their lives, such as a death in the family, parents splitting up, physical or sexual abuse. This triggers emotional eating as a defence mechanism. This kind of mechanism is often called comfort eating. Usually this kind of eating begins in childhood, simply because lots of parents use food as a comfort when things have gone wrong. For instance, you fall over and you're given a candy bar. You go to the doctors for an injection and you're given a lollipop to make you feel better. Unfortunately, comfort eating is only a temporary solution and after the treat is over, whatever you're feeling is still there. If you think this is you, then you need to discuss how you're feeling with someone you trust. If there is no-one in your life you feel you can do this with, then you need to seek outside confidential help (see page 125).

GETTING TO KNOW YOURSELF

The first step in learning to eat only when you're hungry is to pinpoint exactly what your emotional issues are. One way of doing this is to keep a food diary and write down what emotions make you reach for food. If you can do this just as you're about to eat, or just after, you're likely to get the most reliable information because it will still be fresh in your mind.

Remember to include the following:
• what you chose to eat
• how much you ate

- how you felt before you ate (i.e. what made you reach for food)
- how you feel now

Then try to make a list of the following:
- What makes you happy?
- What makes you sad?
- How do you feel about yourself?
- Are you hard on yourself?
- Are you hard on others?

The purpose of this exercise is to understand more about your feelings. If you understand more about yourself, you'll understand what motivates you to eat when you're not hungry.

8 STEPS TO RECLAIM CONTROL OF YOUR EATING HABITS

1) Before you eat, ask yourself, am I hungry?
Listen to your body and try to work out what it's telling you. Our bodies are great mechanisms and they let us know when to eat and when we've had enough. All you have to do is learn to pay attention to what certain signals mean.

2) Think first
Instead of just throwing something into your mouth, ask yourself if you really want it. Or if you're about to deny yourself food, stop and think. If you are really hungry you will only eat more later.

3) Talk about how you feel

If you have emotional problems that you cannot solve, or have no-one to talk to, think about seeking outside help from a professional (see page 125).

4) Give yourself a break

If you do eat something you consider to be 'bad', don't give yourself a hard time about it. Your whole life is not going to fall apart if you eat a chocolate bar.

5) Don't become too obsessed with eating healthily

Healthy eating is great and it means eating regularly and eating a balanced diet. It doesn't mean watching every single thing you put into your mouth, avoiding

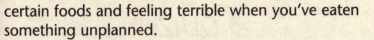

certain foods and feeling terrible when you've eaten something unplanned.

6) Don't let anyone dictate your eating habits

Take control of your own eating habits. Don't let others dictate to you what you should and shouldn't eat and the amounts you should eat. Being made to eat more food than you want is as bad as being denied food that you need.

7) Don't compare your eating habits to others

As eating is such a social event it's easy to compare your portions to those of others. However, our bodies are all made differently and our appetites also work differently. Comparisons mean nothing.

8) Relax when it comes to eating

Eating is meant to be fun. In the UK we have a bad attitude to it. We make something in a hurry, eat it quickly and then go off and do something else. In many other parts of the world eating isn't treated as such an annoyance. It's usually a long drawn out event that is about enjoying both the food and the eating.

● QUIZ ●

DO YOUR EMOTIONS AFFECT THE WAY YOU EAT?

Finish the following sentences

1 When something bad happens in my life I ...
   a) eat more
   b) stop eating
   c) cry

2 I weigh myself ...
   a) once a day
   b) when I feel fat
   c) hardly ever

3 I feel fat ...
   a) constantly
   b) sometimes
   c) never

4 When someone upsets me at home I make myself feel better by ...
   a) eating
   b) skipping meals
   c) shouting at them

5 Diets are a ...
 a) way to become the person you want to be
 b) way to make yourself more unhappy
 c) waste of time

6 When I feel emotional I make myself feel better by ...
 a) eating things I know are 'bad' for me
 b) eating the things I like
 c) being alone

7 Do you seek refuge in food when you feel unloved?
 a) Yes
 b) Sometimes
 c) No

8 When I'm eating I feel ...
 a) safe
 b) guilty
 c) satisfied

Mostly As

It's likely that you use food as a buffer against the world. A way to cushion yourself from things that are unhappy, sad or painful. If you reach for something to eat every time you experience an emotion you can't handle, you need to look at exactly what you're feeling and why. Try talking to someone about how you feel at these times.

Mostly Bs

We all have different ways of coping with upsetting things. You know that food is not the solution when you're feeling bad and battle against eating it. However, if you do succumb every now and then, it's probably because it's one of your coping mechanisms. The way through this is to look at exactly what you're feeling and why.

Mostly Cs

Congratulations – you have pretty healthy attitude to food and your emotions.

CHAPTER FOUR

The diet trap

We are a society obsessed with dieting, it's no wonder that so many of us are worried about our weight and addicted to diets.

It's currently estimated that 90% of British women diet at some point in their lives. These are women who become calorie-obsessed, fat-obsessed and caught in a cycle of weight gain – weight loss – weight gain. If you think you might fall into this category or are fast approaching it, ask yourself the following questions:

1 Are you continually worried about your weight?
2 Are your days classed good or bad depending on how 'fat' or 'thin' you feel?
3 Do you think you'd be happier if you were thinner?
4 Are you obsessed with the calorie and fat content of the food you eat?
5 Do you meticulously weigh up every piece of food?
6 Do you turn down invitations to go out in case you break your diet?
7 Are you always on a diet?
8 Do you look at pictures of food and crave them?

9 Do you weigh yourself every day?
10 Do you think people would like you more if you were thin?

If you've answered yes to more than two of these questions you could be on your way to a life time of dieting.

WHY DO YOU WANT TO LOSE WEIGHT?

Before we even look at why diets are bad news, the first question you have to ask yourself is, why do you want to diet? Is it for health reasons? Has your doctor told you, you need to lose weight? Is it because you feel you are too fat? If so, are you positive you are actually overweight? (It sounds a silly question but many women have such a distorted view of their body that they assume they are overweight when they're not.)

Or are you planning to go on a diet because you think it will improve your life/get you a boyfriend/make you feel happy? If it's one of these reasons, then sadly, losing weight is not the answer. Dieting is not a magical cure for all the things you're unhappy about. Weight gain or loss is just that and nothing else. It doesn't have the power to make your life perfect or happy. So why put yourself through a diet regime if what you're looking for has nothing to do with weight?

Bad reasons to go on a diet

- You want to look like a model
- You want to wear size 10 clothes
- You feel fatter than your friends
- You think boys will fancy you more
- Someone else is making you diet
- Someone else says you're fat
- You feel it's something you should do

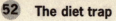

One good reason to go on a diet

You have been told to lose weight for your health.

WAYS PEOPLE TRY TO CONTROL THEIR WEIGHT

Of course, there are many ways people try to lose weight, ways they imagine have nothing to do with dieting. However, a diet – is just a food plan. If you are trying to drop weight by avoiding food in any way, you are actually enforcing a bad food plan on yourself.

Here are some common weight-loss myths:

1. Skipping meals
Does it work? No – skipping meals just makes your body go into starvation mode and cling on to the food you do eat, slowing your metabolism so you burn off calories less quickly.

2. Smoking
Does it work? No – new studies show there is absolutely no correlation between smoking and losing weight. Plus it damages your health.

3. Crash Dieting
Does it work? No – crash dieting can make you put on weight by slowing down your metabolism.

4. Laxative Abuse
Does it work? No – laxative abuse does not lead to weight loss, but does lead to colon and bowel damage.

THE DIET INDUSTRY

"If diets don't work how come there are so many of them about?"

Liz, 13

Dieting is big business. In the UK alone, the slimming industry is worth £2 billion a year, and in America it is worth between 30 and 50 billion dollars.

Check out any book shop and you'll see a huge section on diets. Look closely at the books which promise instant weight loss and instant inch loss and you'll see one fad after another. Go into any chemist and you'll see a shelf full of diet/health products, again all promising instant weight loss success if you drink their special formula or eat their special health bar. Watch morning TV and you'll see consecutive adverts for slimming clubs, slimming foods and slimming bars – all with one objective, to help you lose weight.

You'd think with all these diet foods, slimming classes and miracle diets, everyone would be losing weight left, right and centre but they're not. In fact, in the last 20 years statistics show that as a nation we've become fatter. This has something to do with our lifestyles, a lot to do with the food choices we're making, and unsurprisingly, much to do with dieting itself. The truth is diets make you fat. If they worked, there wouldn't be a need for so many. If you don't believe me, read on.

WHAT DIETING DOES TO YOU IN ADOLESCENCE

"How can dieting be so bad for you? Every one I know does it. It's not like being anorexic or anything."

Annie, 14

Go on a diet and this is how it will make you feel:

- tired
- depressed
- anxious
- food obsessed
- cranky
- lacking in confidence
- tearful

- irritable
- unhappy

Diet frequently and this is what will happen to your body ... you'll

- increase your risk of brittle bones thanks to a lack of calcium
- increase your chances of being shorter, thanks to lack of bone growth
- increase your chances of having an eating disorder
- mess up your metabolism
- affect your menstrual cycle
- affect your fertility
- affect the growth rate of your hair and nails
- diminish your energy levels
- sleep badly
- be constipated

As you can see dieting is bad news, but it's particularly bad for you when you're going through puberty. Food is fuel and the teenage body needs fuel to grow to an adult size. If you diet during puberty you'll not only deprive yourself of energy but also of vital nutrients and minerals the body needs in order to activate your growth spurt.

Remember your body is already programmed with instructions about what it is supposed to do at puberty. It knows it's supposed to prepare you for adult life, therefore, if you interfere with this programme by dieting, the body will respond by going into starvation mode. This means your body becomes twice as efficient in taking every little calorie you eat and storing it as fat.

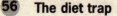

HUNGER AND DIETING

"If I don't eat less food, how am I going to lose weight?"
Suzanne, 14

The dilemma with dieting is, if you don't diet how can you lose weight or control your weight? Well, simply put, your body knows exactly how to control body weight. The problem is dieting confuses the body's signals. Hunger is the signal our brain gives us when we need food. It's the sign our body is short of fuel and needs something to kick start it again.

When you ignore your hunger signals through dieting or only partially eating, you're asking your body to work on less energy.

Think about how you feel when you're hungry and/or on a diet. It's likely to be light headed, irritable, tired and cranky. This is because your body is running on empty. These physical traits are a sign you need to give yourself more food, not less.

If you're worried that eating to satisfy your hunger will make you put on weight, think again. Just as your body has a hunger signal, to say 'feed me!', it also has a signal, to say 'stop!'. If you feed your body properly, it will tell you when it's had enough food. Therefore, you won't want to overeat and will not need to go on a diet.

HOW DIETING LEADS TO WEIGHT GAIN

If you're still not convinced, think about this. Studies now show that more people are overweight, simply because more people are dieting. Dieting, it appears, leads to weight gain for the following reasons.

- **We don't eat enough while on a diet**
  Reducing what we eat affects our metabolism. The metabolism is a clever mechanism and it knows we're getting less calories. When this happens, it slows down, so we actually start to burn calories slower and therefore, gain weight on fewer calories.
- **We eat more when we come off a diet**
  Why do so many women put back the weight they lose after a diet? Simple, they either overeat or go back to unhealthy eating habits. Why? Well, to celebrate and because they feel the deserve a 'treat' after denying themselves food for so long.

The sad truth is that dieting leads to food and weight preoccupation, feelings of failure about yourself, a poor body image, lack of self esteem and depression. Take a look at the following diets and you'll see exactly why they don't work.

MIRACLE DIETS

"I hear about so many different diets I'm not sure which one to go on. My friends are all on the one where you drink only cabbage soup for two weeks."

Helen (16)

Miracle diets should be re-named complete-waste-of-time diets. These diets are not eating plans but ridiculous made up ideas of how a person can drop weight quickly. When you drop weight quickly all you're doing is losing essential muscle mass and water. Therefore, the second you start eating normally again, all that happens is you regain all the lost weight and usually more.

OTHER RIDICULOUS MIRACLE DIETS

- fruit only diet
- brown rice diet
- fat only diet
- bananas diet
- chicken only diet
- vegetable only diet
- junk food diet

MEAL REPLACEMENTS

"I bought this milkshake drink to have for lunch but my teacher says I need more than that and makes me eat lunch."

Helen, 14

Meal replacements are powdered soups or milkshake drinks that provide a low calorie alternative to ordinary meals. Weight is usually regained after the course ends purely because your body knows it needs to replace lost fuel. Meal replacement foods are also a waste of time because they don't educate you to eat properly. Unless you intend to drink milk shakes for

the rest of your life they aren't even worth starting.
What's more, our bodies are made to eat meals, not
drink a meal in a glass. Why replace food, when you
can eat and still be healthy?

CRASH DIETS

*"I sometimes fast because I've heard it's a good way to
lose weight. My sister says it's dangerous – is she
right?"*

Hannah, 13

Apart from being very dangerous to your health,
starving your body of food means you are also
starving it of vital minerals and nutrients. Crash diets
always fail because the body is not stupid. It knows
when it's being deprived of fuel and automatically
slows down your metabolism.

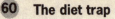

FOOD COMBINING

"How about that diet where you don't eat meat and potatoes together? I think it's something about mixing carbohydrate and protein".

Jilly, 14

This works on the principle that eating acid-forming proteins and starchy carbohydrates at the same time can make you unhealthy and overweight. The basic idea underneath all this is that the digestive system cannot handle a mix of different food groups. This is completely untrue and therefore another waste of time.

LIQUID ONLY DIETS

Highly dangerous and lead to fainting, dizziness and nausea. Also the weight is regained as soon as you start eating again.

CALORIE OBSESSION

"My friends and I are all calorie obsessed. I can't eat anything any more without checking the label and making sure it fits into my 1000 calorie a day diet. It's awful I feel guilty if I eat something bad for me and yet, I crave it if I don't. What's wrong with me?"

Sarah, 17

If your body is craving food when you're on a diet then you are not eating enough. We all need a different amount of calories, (which are a way of measuring how much energy we get from food) and this changes daily and at different times of the month. On some days you might be happy eating a lot of food, and on others less. Counting calories is a waste of time. Therefore, if you want to know how much to eat, listen to your body's signals.

SLIMMING PILLS

"I heard about a new slimming pill in the paper. They said you can lose two stone in a month by taking it. Is this true?"

Dawn, 14

Some pharmaceutical and health companies have come up with perhaps the most persuasive ways of trying to lose weight – pills. Fat burning pills, appetite suppressants, miracle herbs and wonder plants – all designed to help you lose weight. The list is endless and they all promise the same thing – you can lose weight without dieting. All you have to do is hand over lots of money and swallow this!

It's nonsense and these companies get away with it because they know people are desperate to lose weight. If someone offers you diet pills, especially if you're a teenager, don't take them. They will not work and may even make you ill. Some of these products cause diarrhoea and gastrointestinal problems. The more reputable tablets like Orlistat (only available from your doctor) are for people who are clinically obese. And, for the record, it s not a miracle pill, because the people taking it still have to diet, otherwise the pill will not work.

MEN AND DIETING

"I am fat and want to diet but my family just laughs when I say this. My brothers tease me and say it's a girl thing. And my mum thinks I'm being silly. What can I do?"

Jack, 14

It's amazing how many of us grow up with strong messages in the home about what women do, and what men do, with regards to food. It's scary, but the popular message seems to be that boys should eat and girls shouldn't. This is probably why twice as many women as men are dieting.

Fewer men diet, not because they're all at a healthy weight, but simply because fewer men feel the need to improve their body image. Even if they do need (or want) to lose a little weight, men aren't encouraged to go on diets or cut back on certain foods. However, it's important to realise that eating and weight issues can be hard for guys too. The pressures on men are growing and many men and boys worry that they don't have the ideal male physique.

WHEN YOU DO NEED TO DIET

"I know diets are bad for you and I know you should be happy with the way you are, but I really am fat. I weigh 12 stones and I need to lose weight, My mum reckons I'll grow out of it, but I'm worried I won't."

Victoria, 14

Of course, there are certain instances when losing weight is necessary, especially if your weight is affecting your health. If you are overweight and have been told by a doctor that you need to lose weight, he should give you a tailor-made eating plan that should help you to lose weight.

FROM DIETS TO EATING DISORDERS

According to a 1990 study on the Abnormal Eating Attitudes of London Schoolgirls, a dieting girl is eight times more likely to suffer from an eating disorder than a girl who has never dieted.

Experts believe this is because, dieting leads to further dieting, bingeing, crash dieting, restrictive eating techniques and then possibly eating disorders. As you'll see in the next chapter, there is only a fine line between dieting and an eating disorder.

CHAPTER FIVE

Bigger problems

It is estimated that between 60,000 and 120,000 women currently suffer from eating disorders in the UK. At least 5000 of these people are under 16. An eating disorder is basically a psychological condition whereby a person uses food and body size to try to control underlying problems in their life.

Anorexia, bulimia and compulsive eating are perhaps the best-known eating disorders, because they are potentially life threatening and cripple – literally – millions of young people world-wide. Obesity and being addicted to diets are equally painful problems, and also ones in which the sufferer often struggles silently.

If you're someone who is currently suffering from an eating disorder, you'll know how scary it is to feel out of control about your eating. Maybe you are so scared that you can't even admit you have a problem to yourself, or feel so disgusted and repelled by the way you look, that you can no longer leave your house. If this is you, don't despair. With help and support you *can* get better.

WHAT CAUSES AN EATING DISORDER?

"I used to be fat, but my mum let me go on a diet and now I like it that people say I'm thin. I don't think I am thin enough, but I know I'm not fat."

Lena, 10

"I think my stomach sticks out and my bottom is too big. My friends say this isn't true but I know it is because they are all much smaller than me."

Carys, 11

"My dad has called me fatty since I was seven years old. Now my brothers do it too. My mum sticks up for me, but also says if I lost weight they'd like me more. I feel like I am such a big let down to them all."

Donna, 14

"I don't think people like me because I am fat. No-one likes fat people do they? I'd do anything to be thin, because then everything would be fine. I'd have friends who liked me and boys who fancied me. I bet even my parents would stop being mean to me."

Vic, 13

There are no simple answers to what causes an eating disorder. In most cases it's a combination of different factors which cause a person to become ill. What is known is that some people are more vulnerable to eating disorders than others.

Perfectionism

Perfectionists or rather people who have unrealistic expectations of themselves and others – are more prone to becoming ill. This is because people like this feel inadequate and worthless no matter what they achieve. Everything in their lives becomes about 'being better' and often the pursuit of thinness is a part of this.

Does my bum look big in this?

Control

Other people have eating disorders because they want to avoid something painful in their lives – perhaps a family problem or sexuality. Becoming locked in the behaviour patterns of a disorder helps them to bring an element of control to their lives.

Family Triggers

There has been a lot written and said about the role of families and eating disorders. What is known is that some people's families are overprotective and sometimes rigid in the way they deal with problems and conflict. When this occurs some people try to resolve their problems through what they do and don't eat.

Being Female

Girls are disproportionally affected by eating disorders because of the cultural demands on them for thinness. Men by contrast are still encouraged to be strong looking and may equate 'thin' with weak. Ninety to ninety-five per cent of people with eating disorders are female, although figures for male anorexia and bulimia are on the rise and currently stand at around five to ten per cent.

External Problems

Sometimes, external problems can trigger an eating disorder. For instance, bullying, sexual abuse, the break up of a relationship or moving home.

THE RED FLAGS OF AN EATING DISORDER

- A desperate preoccupation with weight, shape, food, calories and dieting.
- Overly and negatively fixating on looks.
- Imagining problems would be solved by being thin.
- An excessive and rigid exercise regime.
- Avoiding situations where food is present.
- Letting food and eating overshadow everything you do.

- Desire to eat alone.
- Abnormal fear of weight gain.
- Extreme concern about the body after eating 'bad' foods.

ANOREXIA

"I'm not sure when I first became anorexic, but I do know I've always thought I was fat. But I think it might have really started when we moved to a new town. I made quite a few friends, but one day I overheard them saying I was pretty but fat. I felt so ashamed and disgusted with myself. I always knew I was repulsive but until that moment I never realised other people did too."

Rachel, 14

Anorexia affects 1 in 150 teenage girls. It is defined as a life-threatening psychological disorder and is thought to have the highest rate of mortality for a psychiatric condition. Approximately 15% of sufferers die as a result of it.

Anorexia is often initiated by normal dieting which spirals out of control, until the whole object of eating becomes a means of coping with stress. Some anorexics eat hardly anything, surviving on tiny morsels of food; while others binge and purge.

However, anorexia nervosa is a disease which is about more than excessive dieting. A sufferer can starve herself to the point of death (many weigh less than 85% of a healthy weight) without realising that she is

thin. In her mind she is always fat.
Sufferers may also embark upon
vigorous exercise regimes and
weigh themselves several times a
day – their whole lives become
centred around food and weight.
Anorexia is in fact a cry for help
and the sufferer needs professional
support. It's a destructive way of
trying to deal with problems and
a way of trying to control a life
you don't understand.

It is extremely difficult to
acknowledge you need help when
you have anorexia, and being
forced to eat by other people is not a solution.
Help can come in various forms and from various
people. If you want to seek help you can go to your
doctor or you can contact the Eating Disorders
Association, Sackville Place, 44–48 Magdalen Street,
Norwich, Norfolk NR3 1JE. Tel: 01603 621414. They
offer help and advice to sufferers and their family and
friends.

Why anorexia makes you ill

An average teenage girl need to consume at least
2000 calories a day in order to sustain the necessary
changes the body undertakes during puberty. An
average teenage boy needs slightly more than this.
Starvation and very low calorie diets interfere with this
process and can stop growth altogether.

If you are someone who eat less than 1000 calories a day (one normal meal a day) then you are starving your body of energy, nutrients and vital vitamins and minerals.

How to spot someone with anorexia

It can be hard to be a friend/sister/brother/parent of someone suffering from an eating disorder because seeing a friend so ill and in need of help can make you feel both helpless and angry as well as concerned and anxious.

If you suspect someone you know has an eating disorder, watch out for the following signs:

- Skipping meals
- Lying about what they eat
- Dramatic weight gain or loss
- Obsessive exercising
- Going to the bathroom directly after each meal.

Remember, eating disorders always get worse if they are not treated. Treatment is based around resolving underlying problems and may involve family therapy.

SYMPTOMS OF ANOREXIA

- Depression
- Anxiety
- Distorted body image – seeing oneself as fat even when emaciated
- Hyperactivity
- Constipation
- Shortness of breath
- Cold hands and feet
- Hair loss

THE RESULTS OF ANOREXIA

- A lack of periods
- Muscle wasting
- Abdominal bloating
- Constipation
- Dry skin
- Appearance of fine, downy hair.
- Fainting, dizziness and insomnia
- Heart, kidney and stomach damage
- Panic attacks
- Bone mineral loss, leading to osteoporosis (brittle bones)
- Low blood pressure
- Bowel damage
- Irregular heart beat

BULIMIA

"I am a bulimic. I think about food all the time and yet whenever I eat I end up making myself sick because I can't bear the thought of putting on weight. Later I get starving again, and eat more food, which only makes me feel more disgusted with myself, making me be sick all over again."

Louisa, 17

"My sister is bulimic. I hear her being sick in the toilet after we have dinner. I am supposed to tell my mum when she does this, but I don't because I don't want to get her into trouble."

Becky, 12

Bulimia affects 3 in every 100 women, which means it's more common than anorexia. As an eating disorder, it can also be fatal but, unlike anorexia, it can often go unnoticed because a bulimic sufferer often looks as if they are maintaining a healthy weight.

Bulimia is sometimes known as the binge/purge syndrome. This is because people who are bulimic eat then make themselves sick in order to control their weight. Some sufferers don't eat for days, then consume huge amounts of food in a very short time, only to vomit it all up. Abuse of laxatives and diuretics are other methods bulimics use to try and control their weight.

Unlike anorexics, bulimics tend to be slightly older (late teens) and have slightly different personalities to anorexics. They tend to be more out-going and impulsive, often hiding how they feel beneath their apparent 'happiness'.

Why bulimia makes you ill

Like anorexia. bulimia is life-threatening because it destroys the body's vital organs. As well as consuming calories to sustain the necessary changes the body undertakes during puberty, teenagers need vital vitamins, minerals and nutrients to help their bodies grow properly. Bingeing and purging interfere with this process and can stop growth all together.

How to spot someone with bulimia

If you suspect someone you know has Bulimia watch out for the following signs:

- Skipping meals
- Lying about what they eat
- Obsessive exercising
- Lengthy and frequent visits to the bathroom
- Excessive fluid intake (this makes vomiting easier)
- Stomach cramps
- Depression
- Vomiting blood
- Bloodshot eyes
- Loss of tooth enamel, leading to decay
- Broken blood vessels
- Dry, flaky skin
- Exhaustion
- Sore throats

- Constipation
- Indigestion

THE RESULTS OF BULIMIA

- Puffy face caused by swollen glands in face and neck
- Irregular heartbeats
- Exhaustion
- Muscle weakness
- Persistent stomach cramps
- Bowel damage

MEDICAL CONSEQUENCES OF BULIMIA

- Fainting, dizziness, depression and insomnia
- Heart, kidney and stomach damage
- Panic attacks
- Dehydration
- Tooth decay
- Bowel damage
- Irregular heartbeat

How to help someone with anorexia or bulimia

- Read up about the disorder. Once you know more about it, you'll be more able to help.
- Try to discuss other things besides weight, food and exercise.
- Avoid making comments about the person's appearance. Mentioning weight loss may be taken as a positive and comments about weight gain as a negative.
- Do not force a person to eat.

- Do not try emotional blackmail.
- Offer support.

If you think you have anorexia or bulimia

- Try to talk to someone
- See your doctor
- Contact the Eating Disorder Association
  01603 621414 – helpline
  01603 765050 – youth line

COMPULSIVE EATING

" My mum is a compulsive eater. I don't know much about it, except that it makes her cry and makes my dad mad. I want to help her but how?"

Nina, 14

Any eating disorder is an expression of a deep emotional conflict and compulsive eating is no different. Also known as binge eating disorder, compulsive overeating is a condition where people engage in frequent binges, but, unlike the bulimic, they do not purge (by vomiting) afterwards. Binges are followed by intense feelings of guilt and shame.

Contrary to what some people may think, compulsive eaters are not greedy. People who suffer from this may be overweight or they may look slim and even thin. Compulsive eaters feel unable to regulate their food intake, for them the mere thought of food is a continuous nightmare. They feel powerless when faced with food and eat more when they feel depressed, upset, angry or anxious. At these times any foods can and will be eaten regardless of the time of day or how hungry the person is.

How to spot a compulsive eater

SYMPTOMS

- Depression
- Feelings of guilt and shame
- Antisocial behaviour
- Obesity

RESULTS OF COMPULSIVE EATING

- Poor circulation
- Shortness of breath
- Poor Complexion
- Wind
- Bad breath

MEDICAL CONSEQUENCES OF COMPULSIVE EATING

- High blood pressure
- High cholesterol
- Diabetes
- Heart Disease

DIET ADDICTION

"My friends and I go from one diet to another. The latest one is about eating vegetable soup every day, and nothing else. It sounds extreme but it's apparently made up by a hospital, so it must be good."

Lisa, 15

"My mum and I have tried all the diets and still we can't lose weight. It's so depressing."

Sarah, 13

"I have every diet book that's out. I've tried eating brown rice for two weeks, eating only fruit and vegetables and even eating only once a day. It's all rubbish, I've only ever lost about 4lbs."

Maria, 15

Continual restriction of what you eat means that you automatically start to become preoccupied with it. It's human nature to want something you know you shouldn't have.

Like all eating disorders, diet addiction can and does take over your life.

ADDICTED TO EXERCISE

"I think my best friend is addicted to exercise. The second we've eaten she insists on going for a run. She says she feels guilty if she doesn't do this after every meal."

Mel, 13

Like any thing in life, it is possible to become too focused on exercising. If you answer yes to any of the following, it's likely you are over-exercising and need to examine your attitude to exercise and talk to someone about how you feel.

Do you ...

- feel depressed and anxious if you can't exercise ?
- feel you have to exercise every time you eat something?
- insist on doing hundreds of repetitions of exercises like stomach crunches and press ups?
- exercise even when you're injured?
- feel fat if you miss an exercise session?
- not enjoy exercise but make yourself do it because you're afraid not to?
- imagine your body would be disgusting if it wasn't for exercise?
- make yourself do much more exercise than you need to do?

OBESITY

"I know I am extremely over weight, probably even obese. I am 5' 2" and I weigh nearly 13 and a half stone. People think I like the way I am, but I don't. I hate myself. I hate my body. I hate being fat. I would give anything to lose weight, but I can't do it. I've just got too much to lose."

Ellie, 14

"My mum is obese and people are so mean to her. They call her names and say cruel things. It's not her fault. She tries to lose weight I know she does. I love her so much, it really hurts when people are mean about her."

Lou, 12

Obesity is the medical definition for people who weigh more than 20% of their recommended healthy weight. The Department of Health survey published in January 1998, showed that 16% of men and 17% of women in England are now obese. What's more, the latest data from the National Study of Health and Growth shows that over one-fifth of children are now overweight and about 1 in 10 are obese.

Although obesity is genetically predisposed, most people become obese as a result of bad life style choices, like not exercising. The problem with obesity is the health risks. When you're obese you're at increased risk of diabetes, heart disease, high blood pressure, and two to three time more likely to have depression and die prematurely.

It sounds scary and this is why obesity is one of the few reasons why a person should lose weight and change what they eat. If you think you are seriously overweight, you should see your doctor. (Don't bother with weight charts, what your friends say or weighing scales.) If your doctor thinks you do need to lose weight, he or she will give you a diet sheet that will help you to eat properly and healthily, and may talk to you about exercise and why it's essential for good health. This is the safe way to lose weight.

FIVE STEPS TO LOSING WEIGHT

1 See your doctor to find out if you need to lose weight.
2 Don't put yourself on a restrictive diet where you crave food you cannot have. Instead find an eating plan that works for you.
3 Start exercising – see chapter 8 for ideas on how to make it easier!
4 Don't think it's pointless to try to lose weight, believe you can do it.
5 Ask your family and friends for support.

WHAT TO DO IF YOU THINK YOU MAY HAVE AN EATING DISORDER

- Admit you have a problem to yourself
- See your doctor
- Tackle your underlying problems by seeking help from a counsellor
- Contact the Eating Disorders Association
  01603 621414 – helpline
  01603 765050 – youth line
- If you are overeating contact Overeaters Anonymous – 01426 984674

CHAPTER SIX

Healthy eating

What does eating healthily mean to you? Does it mean eating like a sparrow and refusing to touch an endless list of your favourite things – chocolate bars, cakes, biscuits, cheese? Or does it mean vegetables, vegetables and more vegetables? If you think it means either of the above, it's time to change your attitude. Healthy eating is about maintaining balance in your diet, not swapping one kind of food regime for another.

The fact is, the emphasis on 'good' and 'bad' foods has backfired. People focusing on the 'badness' of some foods has not stopped weight gain, dieting, eating disorders or obesity. And instead of helping people to make better choices about what to eat, it's made people think obsessively about food, and deprive themselves of what they really want.

Healthy eating is about eating a full range of foods. It is one of the most important ways we can help ourselves to feel energised and good about our bodies. What's more, if you eat the right balance of food, you needn't ever worry about your weight.

HOW HEALTHY ARE YOUR FOOD CHOICES?

If you're not sure if you have an unhealthy attitude to healthy eating, ask yourself the following questions:

1 Do you feel better if you eat a salad instead of a burger?
2 Do you make judgements on people by what they're eating?
3 Do you divide foods into good and bad?
4 Do you feel guilty if you've eaten something you consider to be unhealthy?
5 Are you completely focused on healthy eating?
6 Have you removed all fatty foods from your diet?
7 Are you picky about the foods you eat?
8 Do you feel panicky if you have to go to someone's house for dinner and you don't know what they're serving?
9 Do you choose fat-free products so you won't put on weight?
10 Have you ever thrown food away because you're afraid you'll eat it all?

More than two yes answers and the chances are you need to take another look at your view of healthy eating.

What healthy eating isn't

"Why are people always saying fat, sugar and salt are bad for you? How are you meant to cut them all out of your diet? I want to eat healthily but it's so confusing."

Tracey, 14

Contrary to popular belief, healthy eating *doesn't* mean cutting out all your favourite foods, buying more expensive foods, denying yourself what you like, and/or eating the same things over and over. It also doesn't mean feeling hard done by after a meal.

Healthy eating having a healthy attitude to food, so that your feelings aren't affected by what you eat. If you are obsessed with the food you consume, picky to the point of annoyance, and strict about what you will and won't allow yourself to eat, you're not a healthy eater.

What healthy eating *does* mean

According to a Health Education Authority survey 34% of young adults think that healthy foods are 'too boring'. But healthy eating doesn't mean eating just vegetables and fruit. Healthy eating means eating a balanced diet, including foods you like and not labelling some foods 'bad' and others 'good'.

GOOD FOODS AND BAD FOODS

Hundreds of articles are published in the papers every day about healthy eating and what to eat and what not to eat. 'Eat eggs', one paper says, 'No, don't', says another. 'Pasta makes you fat', claims one, 'Pasta makes you thin,' responds another. Chocolate, junk food, and cheese have all got a bad press too. These reports make us divide foods up into good and bad. The problem with thinking about food like this is that, you immediately place yourself in the following vicious circle.

You imagine the food to be bad – so you deny yourself it – then you crave it – so you give in and eat it – then you imagine you've done something wrong, and so you end up feeling guilty and banning it again.

You also start to imagine a bad food has nothing to offer you. The fact is there are no good and bad foods. Burgers and chips aren't bad, chocolate isn't bad, ice cream isn't bad. It's really a question of how often you eat these things. If you realise that chocolate takes longer to work off than bread, it doesn't mean bread is 'better' and you should deny yourself chocolate. It does, however, mean you should be aware of what you're eating and educate yourself about how often you should eat certain food.

Moderation is the key here. This means a balanced diet of a little bit of what you like, a little bit of what you should eat and a little bit of vegetables and fruit. By eating a variety of foods like this, you can eat whatever you want, when you want it, and not worry about weight gain. Of course, if you eat loads of junk food, plus all the things that are supposedly good for you, you will gain weight, simply because you have upped your food intake and not balanced out your diet. Below is a run down of some of the food considered to be 'bad' and why they're not the real enemy.

Junk food

Like it or not, fast food is part of our culture and it isn't going away, so forcing yourself to avoid it is a waste of time. If you eat at fast food places, do so in moderation and it won't hurt your health. Surprisingly, these foods do provide nutrition, especially protein, iron, vitamins and fibre. For example, a burger contains iron, and vitamins essential for growth.

Pasta and bread

Pasta, bread, potatoes and other starches are not fattening and bad for you. If they were, the Health Education Authority wouldn't be recommending that you ate at least six to eight servings a day. Usually it's what you top it with that causes weight gain.

Red meat

The fat content of red meat isn't higher than that of chicken or turkey; it's also a better source of iron, making it a healthy food to eat.

Sugar

Sugar has a bad press but our bodies need a little for energy. Eating it in is not only pleasurable but better for you than avoiding it altogether. Bear in mind sugar doesn't have to be the processed kind – it occurs naturally in fruit and honey.

Fat

Sure, it's high in calories but we still need to have fat in our diets (see below).

BAN THOSE EATING RULES

We're all led to believe if we deny ourselves food we will gain a healthy eating regime, yet restrictive eating always backfires. So if you have any of the following rules in your life, and want to be a healthy eater, start by banning them.

1   *'No sweets and cakes.'*
A bad move because it will only make you want them even more and when you do eat them you're likely to eat much more of them.

2   *'No junk food.'*
Impossible and impractical to keep to, especially if you're going out with friends. Be realistic and eat fast food in moderation.

3   *'No snacking.'*
A common family food rule, yet if you feel hungry you should eat. The body is designed to get hungry every three to four hours, not just at meals times. If you need to eat, then it's your body's signal you need energy. (You could try fruit instead of crisps.)

4   *'Finish all your food.'*
If you no longer feel hungry you should stop eating.

5   *'Girls don't have seconds.'*
Rubbish – what more can we say?

6   *'Boys need to eat more.'*
Some boys do and some boys don't, just as some girls do and some girls don't.

7   *'Avoid dessert at all costs.'*
Only if you're full and don't want it.

8   *'Overweight people eat more.'*
Not necessarily. Studies show weight gain is caused by an unbalanced diet and lack of exercise.

What's wrong with fat?

 "I've heard that eating fat makes you fat. I want to give it up but my mum says I need it to grow. Who's right?"

Andrea, 13

We all need fat in our diets. Fat is essential for a variety of functions, including digestion, immunity and hormone production. What's more, fat in food is actually concentrated energy (measured in calories). We need this energy for growth, to keep our bodies working properly and to enable us to do the things we want to do.

If you deny yourself fat, especially at puberty, your hormone production will shut down, oestrogen will not be produced and your periods will stop. Your bones will also be starved of oestrogen, making them prone in later life to osteoporosis.

However, the reason why such a fuss is made over fat is because it contains more than double the amount of calories than you find in protein and carbohydrates. Our bodies are designed to convert all the food we eat into energy, but if too much energy is consumed it will convert the excess food into excess fat on your body.

Ideally fat should provide a third of all the calories in our diet, but most people get too many calories from fat and not enough from proteins and carbohydrates. So make sure you eat some fat, without over doing it.

SHOULD WE BE EATING FAT-FREE?

Contrary to popular belief, fat-free food doesn't mean you can scoff as much as you want. It is still high in calories, which means that if you overeat it on a regular basis you'll put on weight because you'll be consuming too many calories.

LOW FAT ICE CREAM

WHAT FAT TO EAT

There are two different kinds of fat, unsaturated and saturated fat. Saturated fat comes from animal fats and tends to be hard (e.g. butter or lard); unsaturated fat is found in vegetables and fish oils and tends to be softer. This fat is also known as polyunsaturated and mono-unsaturated.

It is recommended by the Health Education Authority that saturated fat should be replaced with unsaturated fat. This is because a diet high in saturated fat leads to a variety of illnesses, including heart disease. The easiest way to change is to use products that have olive oil, fish oil or oil from plant sources not animal sources.

What is cholesterol?

Cholesterol is a fatty substance that is found naturally in all people. It is essential to a number of body processes such as the formation of hormones and body cells. Cholesterol is also an important ingredient of bile which aids the digestion of fatty foods in our bodies. There is so much talk about cholesterol because even though it is essential to sustain life, too much in the blood can lead to serious health problems such as heart attacks.

Very high cholesterol levels are usually only found in adults after a lifetime of eating too much fat. High levels occur from eating saturated fats and fatty products such as dairy food, biscuits, cakes, eggs and sausages. Eating well when you're young will lessen your chances of high cholesterol.

What's wrong with salt?

Salt is something that occurs naturally in our food and it plays an important role in controlling the fluid balance in our bodies. It also works to make sure our muscles and nerves work properly. However, it is thought that too much salt can lead to high blood pressure which may make a person more susceptible to heart attacks. The amount of salt we actually need is only three-quarters of a teaspoon a day. This is consumed naturally without even adding salt to food.

Cutting down on salt in food is easy because all you have to do is stop adding it. It will taste odd at first but your taste buds will quickly adjust and the natural flavour of food will take its place.

What about carbohydrates?

Carbohydrates are broken into two types – sugar and starch. A healthy diet is one that has more starchy carbohydrates (which are very good for you) and fewer sugars. Starch is found in bread, cereals, pasta, rice and some fruits. Sugars are found in syrup, jam, treacle, honey, raw cane sugar, glucose, dextrose and fructose (check labels to see) and fizzy drinks. None of these sugars have any nutrients or give your body anything apart from energy. Again if you consume too much and don't exercise, the body will store the excess as fat on your body.

Why fibre is essential

Fibre is the name for a group of carbohydrates found in beans, brown bread, brown, rice, potatoes, wholemeal pasta and vegetables. Fibre fills you up and can help protect you against digestive problems including cancer of the bowel, which is one of the most common cancers in Britain.

ALL HEALTHY DIETS CONTAIN:

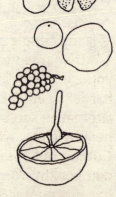

Everyday ...

3–5 Servings of fruit and vegetables
It may sound boring but fruit and vegetables are excellent foods because they have a variety of nutrients, vitamins and minerals stored within.

8–10 Servings of breads/cereal/ rice and/or pasta
Nutritionists recommend a diet made up of at least 50 % carbohydrates.

2–4 Servings of protein
Protein in this group is classified as chicken, red meat, nuts and eggs.

2–3 Servings of Fat and Calcium
This is found in milk, cheese and yoghurt.

A little bit of what you like

- *Examples of servings are: one piece of fruit; one slice of bread; ½ cup of cooked pasta; 2oz of cheese; 1oz cooked vegetables; ⅓ pint of milk; 9 fluid oz of yoghurt; a handful of nuts.*

IS BEING A VEGETARIAN MORE HEALTHY?

"I want to become a vegetarian because I know it will help me lose weight. My mum says this is rubbish, but I'm sure I'm right."

Jenny, 14

Many people assume vegetarians are more healthy than meat-eaters, but it really depends on what you eat. If you are a vegetarian, you have to try even harder to eat a balanced diet because you have to find alternative sources protein, an essential part of a healthy diet – which non-vegetarians get from meat. Cutting out meat does not automatically make your diet healthy. Many vegetarians also find they consume too much fat in their diets (e.g. from eating a lot of cheese) and so have to be more inventive when it comes to making meals.

30 ways to healthy eating

1 Learn to enjoy what you eat.

2 Eat when you feel hungry, even if it's not a specific mealtime.

3 Be aware that your appetite will be different every day and sometimes you'll want to eat more than at other times.

4 Always have a little of what you like.

5 Remember different foods supply different mixtures of minerals and vitamins for your body.

6 Avoid eating one thing over and over because no one single food can supply what you need.

7 Bear in mind that nutritional requirements increase as we go through adolescence. The estimated daily energy requirement for teenage girls aged 11 – 14 years is at least 2000 calories a day and for girls aged 14–18 at least 2110 calories and slightly more for boys.

8 Body weight is determined by the amount of energy eaten compared to the amount of energy the body uses. Over 50% of people in the UK are overweight mainly because they don't exercise.

9 Try not to overeat and if you do, look at why you might be.

10 Forget miracle diets. Weight loss can be maintained by exercising and eating a healthy balanced diet.

11 Do not skip meals.

12 Make sure you eat plenty of fresh fruit and vegetables.

13 Talk to your mum or dad (whoever does most of the cooking) about healthier ways you can cook together, for example, grilling instead of frying foods.

14 Add a variety of food to your diet so you don't get bored.

15 Don't eat fat-free products, instead just eat a little of something in its natural form.

16 Experiment with food. Don't just write off something you think sounds horrible, try it first.

17 Don't be fanatical about what you eat.

18 Worry about your own not anybody else's.

19 Trust your body's needs.

20 Allow yourself to feel hungry so you can recognise what it feels like.

21 Eat breakfast – eating kick starts the metabolism, meaning you'll burn more energy than those who skip it.

22 Drink lots of water, at least 8 to 12 glasses a day. Your body needs water not only to digest food, but also to detox your system.

23 Make sure you eat enough carbohydrates. The body burns up carbohydrates (like pasta and bread) faster than any other food, with only a tiny percentage turned into fat.

24 Make your meals last at least 20 minutes. This is because the brain takes longer than the stomach to realise you're full. Slow down and you won't overeat.

25 Don't go shopping for food when you're hungry – you'll be more likely to suggest foods you know aren't so healthy for you.

26 Suggest to your parents that you try to eat more fresh food, as many pre-cooked foods have a high saturated fat content.

27 When you're out with friends, or at a sweet shop, read food before you eat.

28 Be careful where you eat. Studies show people who eat in front of the TV consume more and at a faster rate than people who eat round a table.

29 Before you eat, get into the habit of trying to recognise whether or not you are hungry and how hungry you actually are.

30 Don't eat fat on meat and skin on chicken as these are extremely high in saturated fat.

CHAPTER SEVEN

Your self esteem

THE SELF IMAGE TEST

1 How often do you look in a mirror?
  a) Only if you're passing one. (10)
  b) Never! Your reflection makes you feel sick. (0)
  c) As much as you can. You want to make sure you look good. (5)

2 How often do you weigh yourself?
  a) Never (0)
  b) Every day (5)
  c) Only when you have to (10)

3 What word best sums up your body?
  a) Okay (10)
  b) Fat (5)
  c) Ugly (0)

4 What's the worst thing someone could say about you?
  a) You have a horrible body (0)

b) You're stupid (10)

c) You're nasty (5)

5 If you could swap bodies with someone else who would it be?

a) A model (0)

b) An actress you admire (5)

c) Someone you know (10)

6 What do you do when you're having a 'bad hair' day?

a) Go out, but feel terrible all day (5)

b) Try to think positively about yourself (10)

c) Stay at home (0)

7 Would you change anything major about yourself?

a) Yes, my whole self (0)

b) Yes, my body (5)

c) Nothing major (10)

Add up your scores marked in brackets after each answer and look below for the results.

0 – 20

You have the classic traits of someone who has low self esteem and a bad body image. But all is not lost! You can change your attitude to yourself and your body. All you have to do is carry on reading.

25 – 55

Even though you're quite adept at hiding those negative feelings, you know you're pretty hard on yourself. If you want to shape up your self esteem, this is the right chapter for you.

60 – 80

Well done – your self esteem is pretty good! However, if a part of you still imagines the worst now and then, you can benefit from reading on.

WHAT IS SELF ESTEEM?

Self esteem is basically the way you feel about yourself. People with high self esteem feel good about themselves and know that not having a perfect body or an ideal weight is okay. If you have good self esteem, you know to treat your body with respect.

Unfortunately, lots of people don't feel this way about themselves because negative feelings about weight have eaten away at their self esteem. If you don't believe me, ask yourself this: how many times have you got up in the morning and judged how you felt about yourself by the size of your stomach? Or considered how attractive you were by whether or not an article of clothing fitted properly?

If this sounds familiar you're not alone. Many, many people have bad self esteem, a distorted body image and feelings of self disgust about themselves.

DO YOU HAVE A DISTORTED VIEW?

While occasional feelings of dissatisfaction are normal, if you have a distorted view of yourself, you may have a more serious problem in the making. If you answer yes to three or more of the following questions, the chances are you need to start working on your beliefs and self esteem right now.

1 Do you frequently call yourself negative weight-related names?
2 Do you get depressed when you go out because everyone looks thinner or curvier than you?
3 Do you think people would like you more if you weighed less or more?
4 Do you disregard compliments but hang on to insults?
5 Do you wear baggy clothes to cover up?
6 Do you pretend you're happy the way you are?

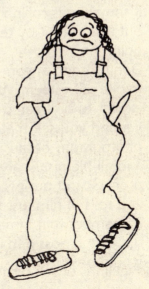

HOW TO STOP NEGATIVE MESSAGES

As well as tackling family problems in the way we've seen in previous chapters, here are some other things you can do to stop negative messages:

- If you don't like a particular label a friend has given you, be assertive and say so. Laughing along and trying to ignore it doesn't work, it just makes people think they can tease you even more.

- Remember it's boring to have to bolster someone else's confidence all the time. If you're someone who keeps asking, "How do I look?" just so you feel secure, don't do it. Instead learn to trust your own opinion.

- If a boy is putting you down, making you feel inadequate and wanting you to change – it's time to deal with him. Any man who won't accept you for who you are (and boys – the same goes for girls!), doesn't deserve you. Take control and tell him so.

- If someone is calling you names or bullying you, put a stop to it by telling an adult you trust what's going on.

- Don't forget, anyone (male or female) can have fragile self esteem. Always treat people how you expect to be treated yourself.

- Remind yourself that models looks flawless in photographs because the pictures are touched up, and all blemishes are taken out in the printing process, and professional photographers shoot rolls and rolls of film just to get one perfect shot.

- Remember that fame doesn't equal happiness. If it did all the gossip magazines and tabloid papers would be out of business.

WHY YOU NEED SELF ESTEEM

Having a good body image is important because it's a vital part of your self confidence. If you hate the way you look and feel, then you won't project yourself in a positive way to people you meet. Learning to respect yourself, warts and all, is a way of saying to yourself and other people, 'I'm a great person and I'm worth knowing.' It also stops you from wasting your life in trying to attain a level of perfection which just doesn't exist.

LEARNING TO FEEL GOOD ABOUT YOURSELF

How do you feel about your body and weight? Write down on a piece of paper the first three things that come to your head.

The chances are you will have written some negative things (if you haven't, congratulations! – you don't need to do the next bit of the exercise). Now write three things you love about your body (physical things like the shape of your legs, etc.).

Look at both your lists. Which one was the harder one to write? If you're being honest it was probably the second. This is because most of us are so good at saying mean things about our bodies and focusing on the bits we hate, that we often forget we have good parts too. Sometimes, if we say mean things for long enough we start to really believe there is nothing good to praise. We make comments like, "Oh well, it's personality that counts" – which of course is true but that doesn't mean you can totally write off everything else.

DON'T GIVE UP ON YOUR BODY

Rather than giving up on your body and concentrating on your personality, you need to accept that one part is directly linked to the other. You cannot separate the two no matter how hard you try. The simple fact is, until you learn to respect your body as much as your mind, behaviour and attitudes, you will never truly respect or feel good about yourself.

WHAT BETTER SELF ESTEEM WILL LEAD TO

- Feeling good about your body, even if it's not exactly how you want it to be.
- Not comparing yourself negatively to others and then feeling depressed.
- Not judging your day by how fat/big/small your stomach/nose/breasts were.
- Being aware of how harshly you judge other people's bodies.
- More confidence when you're with other people.
- No more yo-yo dieting, fad diets and mad exercise schemes.
- Not being hurt and over sensitive to people's comments.

MIRROR IMAGE

For some people, looking in the mirror can be a nightmare. It can make them feel depressed, miserable, anxious and even suicidal. It may seem ridiculous to people who have good self images but low self esteem in this area can seriously hold you back in every other area of your life. Imagine having to look the other way every time you saw a mirror, just so you wouldn't have to be reminded of how 'bad' you look.

Now, think of the person who always dreads having their photograph taken and then winces when he or she has to look at the result. This is the person who can never find her best side, can never take a compliment but stores up all the negative things people throw her way and reminds herself of them constantly. This person could very well be you or your best friend, or your mum or all three of you.

MAKING FRIENDS WITH YOUR MIRROR

Horrible as it sounds, if you want to feel good about your body and weight, you have to get used to your reflection. Of course, making friends with the way you look isn't easy but it can be done. All it takes is a bit of practice.

Day One:
Ever noticed how when you first look at a photograph of yourself it appears to look terrible, but when you keep looking at it, it actually starts to look pretty good? Well, this is what happens with your reflection.

The first time you look at yourself, you're flooded with negative messages which distort your view. But, if you keep looking and keep a positive mind, your view of yourself will change. The exercise for today is to start keeping a body journal. Begin by noting down how you feel the first time you look in the mirror.

Day Two:
Look at your reflection for about one minute (don't think about yourself or look for flaws). Start by doing it for about one minute every day and write down how you feel. Remember, choose a mirror where you can see all of yourself (not just your face or your legs), so you get a view of the whole of yourself.

Day Three:
Do the same exercise and this time when you look, as well as writing something down, say something positive about what you see (you don't have to say this aloud). You may feel stupid at first but persevere!

Day Four:
Try to find something different and positive to say to yourself and again keep a note of it.

Day Five:
Increase the time you look from 1 minute to 3 minutes. Observe how your view of yourself is changing (or has changed) and write it down.

Repeat this exercise every time you start to feel negative about yourself.

THROWING AWAY THE SCALES

Do you have weighing scales in your house? How often do you leap on them? Do they make you feel bad about yourself? Do you fear them?

If so, you're not alone. Many people let their weighing scales dictate how they feel about themselves. If this sounds like you, what you have to realise is:

1 Scales cannot measure who and what you are.
2 The average body weight fluctuates between 2 and 3 lbs every day, so there's not much point in constantly weighing yourself.
3 Rather than fixating on what the scales say, take more notice of how your clothes feel.
4 If you really need to lose weight, don't weigh yourself everyday. Choose a particular time once a week to do it and don't aim for a loss of more than 2 lbs a week. Any more than this and you will be starving your body of food.

Step One: Wean yourself off the scales. If you usually get on every day, try changing to every other day. Then once a week, then once a month, until you no longer feel the need to see how much you weigh.

Step Two: Learn to judge your weight by the way you feel about yourself. Do your clothes feel comfortable? Can you climb the stairs without getting breathless?

Step Three: Give your scales away or if they belong to your mum ask her to keep them somewhere where you won't be tempted to climb on them.

Step Four: If you want to judge how big/small/fat/ thin you are, look at yourself in the mirror.

THE INNER CRITIC

The inner critic is that voice that sabotages your confidence. The one that whispers in your ear: "Lose weight", "You're too fat", "You look horrible", "No-one will ever fancy you", "Your bottom's too big".

We've all got a voice like this. It chants what we might have done, what we could have done, and what we should have done. It tells us we're inferior, we look bad and that no matter how hard we try, we just have to try harder and harder.

Unfortunately, these thoughts can be so automatic that you may not even be conscious of them. Or you might think you're being 'realistic' or 'honest' with yourself. Studies show that women are more prone to accept self criticism as true, while men are more likely to challenge their negative thoughts. Lots of these thoughts are created in childhood and adolescence, so this is the time to challenge them, before they get even harder to shake off in later life.

Silencing that inner critic

- Accept that your inner voice is coming from you, not the people you're with, your parents, or even some outside force.
- Once you accept that your voice is part of your insecurity, don't accept what it says, challenge it; say no to it.
- Every time you say something mean to yourself, write it down. After a week look back at what you've said to yourself. Look for patterns, e.g. were you meaner when you felt vulnerable or had PMT?
- Now look at the standards you set yourself. Are they attainable or too high? Replace every negative thought with a positive one.
- Develop an inner coach that spurs you on every time you feel scared or vulnerable. Start by telling yourself why you can do something, not why you can't.
- Focus on your good points. If you can't find one, ask your friends and family to all give you one good point about yourself and write it down for future reference.
- Get rid of all the 'shoulds' in your life. There is

nothing you 'should' do, only things you choose
to do.
• Be patient with yourself. We all have self doubts, but
you can change the way you feel if you give yourself
some time, and work towards it day
by day.

CHANGING WHAT YOU CAN

The first step in dealing with a bad self image is to
realise that there are THINGS YOU CAN CHANGE
and THINGS YOU CAN'T.

Make a list now of all the things you hate about your
body. Then fill in either the second column (THINGS I
CAN CHANGE) or third (THINGS I CAN'T). For
instance if you hate your weight, then that is
something you can change. If you hate your height,
that's something you can't. If you hate your skin
colouring, then that's also something you can't change.

Now, if there are things you hate which you can't
change, this means they are a fundamental part of you.
You now have a choice, either accept them or let them
get you down. Acceptance doesn't mean you have to
be blissfully happy but it does mean you have to stop
blaming all your problems on them.

Now look at the list of things you can change. If you
really want to change these things then you can. It
doesn't mean it won't be hard, take time or even take
effort – the chances are, it'll be all these things and
more!

Remember, change is always hard but people do it all the time.

If you make a decision to change something you dislike remember the following:

- It won't make all your other problems disappear
- It won't happen overnight
- It will be worth it in the end

Above all remember that FEELING GOOD ABOUT YOURSELF HAS NOTHING TO DO WITH LOOKS. Sure, when you feel fit and healthy and are wearing the clothes you want, you feel more attractive. But being attractive comes from inside of us. It's about feeling good about yourself, being positive about your good points, not letting your bad ones get you down and RECOGNISING YOU HAVE LOTS TO OFFER.

CHAPTER EIGHT

Fit for life

"I hate exercise. It's okay for people who are thin, they know they can do stuff and be good at it. But I'm useless so I'd rather not do any."

Sian, 13

Statistics show that as a nation we are getting fatter simply because we don't take enough exercise. The latest government research shows young people in particular are ruining their future health, by watching more TV, doing more sedentary activities like playing computer games, and being driven to school, instead of walking. The simple correlation between an inactive lifestyle like this and weight is simply that the less you move, the more you'll weigh and the less fit you'll be.

If you're at all worried about your weight, exercise is probably the one area you avoid at all costs, when the truth is that it can help you more than you think. However, before you turn off and think this chapter isn't for you, let me point out that the kind of exercise I'm talking about doesn't mean joining the athletics team or doing 500 sit ups before you go to bed. I'm talking about activities you can permanently make part of your everyday life, that will make you feel good about your body, your health and yourself.

Like healthy eating, and maintaining your self esteem, exercise is for life. You cannot just do the above as a means to ends and then go back to your old ways. Becoming healthy is about re-education, a way of changing your lifestyle permanently. It sounds painful but it's not and the benefits it will bring you will not only improve your self esteem but also your health, for life.

WHAT EXERCISE CAN DO FOR YOU

- Improve your confidence
- Improve your health
- Help you to maintain a weight you're happy with
- Give you healthy skin
- Make you feel happy
- Give you more energy
- Stop you from feeling depressed
- Make you feel strong
- Give you a leaner and fitter body
- Increase your chances for better health when you're older
- Prevent heart disease
- Lower your blood pressure
- Prevent some forms of diabetes
- Burn calories
- Slow down the ageing process
- Make you feel more relaxed
- Make you feel more awake

"Why does everyone make such a fuss about exercise? If you can lose weight by dieting surely that's all you need to do?"

Anne, 15

Time and time again, studies have shown that nothing is better for you than regular exercise. Twenty minutes, three times a week is all we're talking about here. This will not only increase your fitness levels but also decrease stress, keep depression away, prevent sleeplessness and increase your all round energy levels. To achieve this kind of fitness you do not have to run, go to step classes or invest in dumbbells and fancy trainers. But you do have to do an aerobic and anaerobic activity at a certain intensity to get the physical benefits you need.

AEROBIC EXERCISE

Aerobic exercise is exercise which requires a lot of oxygen.

Do it regularly and you will:

- Be more energetic, less tired and leaner.
- Have a stronger heart, so it doesn't need to pump as often to pump blood through your body.
- Burn body fat as fuel. This is great if you want to lose weight because body fat will be burnt off and your lean muscle tissue (the stuff that's lost when you crash diet) will stay.
- Reduce your risk of a serious illness and heart disease.

- Increase your metabolism, which means you'll burn off more body fat.
- Increase your endorphin levels. Endorphins are the body's natural pain killers and help to keep you feeling good.

Best aerobic activities

WALKING

This improves cardiovascular (the way your lungs and heart work) strength and muscle strength.

SWIMMING

This improves upper and lower body muscles as well as aerobic strength.

CYCLING

High quality, aerobic exercise that works arms and legs.

How much aerobic exercise you need

- Three to five times a week
- At least 20 mins each session
- To make sure you are working at the right intensity your breathing should be fairly laboured, but you should have enough breath to talk
- Start slowly and gradually and you'll notice the benefits in 4 weeks

ANAEROBIC EXERCISE

Anaerobic exercise is exercise that uses muscle strength rather than oxygen. Anaerobic exercise, or strength training, is good for fitness because it strengthens your bones and tones and shapes your body. It helps you to build up muscles (don't worry, you won't end up looking like a body builder!) that will continue to burn calories even when you're not doing anything. Most people assume you have to lift weights for anaerobic exercise, yet virtually every exercise that uses aerobic energy also uses anaerobic energy.

Do it regularly and you will:

- Feel stronger.
- Burn more calories.
- Have better muscle tone.
- Increase muscle mass which will keep your body healthy.
- Reduce body fat.
- Control blood pressure.

The best anaerobic exercise

Any exercise which increases you muscle strength. This can be any kind of work with weights, swimming, tennis, and/or power walking, where you pump your arms as you walk.

How much anaerobic exercise you need

- Two to three times a week
- For at least 20 mins

- To make sure you are working at the right intensity your movements should be slow, but you should have enough breath to talk
- Start slowly and gradually and you'll notice the benefits in 4 weeks.

A LITTLE BIT IS BETTER THAN NOTHING

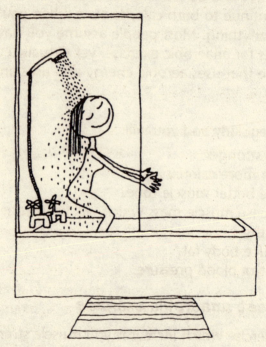

Apart from the obvious weight connection with exercise, being active can change a lot of things in your life. For instance, after doing some kind of exercise many people report feeling less stressed and irritated, and more able to concentrate. They also say they feel better about themselves and their lives.

If you feel daunted by the idea that you have to do it for 20 minutes, 3 times a week, you might be interested to know research shows a little bit of exercise is better for you than none at all. So if you can only manage to do it once a week, that's better than not doing anything.

If you feel that exercise is just too much like hard work, it's time to challenge your attitude to activity and start doing things that you like. Think positively because exercise can save your life.

WHEN YOU HATE PE LESSONS

"I hate exercise. They make us do all kinds of stupid things at school. I'm always thinking up stupid ways to get out of the classes."

Tina, 14

Many of us are put off exercise and sport for life, thanks to our school physical education lessons. Why? Well, because not all of us are made to be good at competitive sports, team games and athletics. However, what you have to realise is, exercise is about more than sport. It's about being active, not about excelling at a specific activity. If you feel humiliated by your PE efforts, maybe have a word with your teacher and see if she'll incorporate different kinds of non-competitive activities into your lessons.

Above all, remember, exercise is a personal issue about becoming healthy and not about being number one.

What's more, even if you hate your school PE lessons and do everything you can to get out of them, remember, you can still be fit by putting more activity into your life. For instance, just because running around a football pitch or netball court isn't your idea of fun, it doesn't mean you have to give up on moving all together. Try and find alternatives to sport, maybe solo activities like cycling where you don't feel pushed to have to beat someone or to do something within a specific time frame.

CHANGING YOUR ATTITUDE

The first step in changing your attitude towards your body and exercise is to work out why you want to change your ways and how you're going to achieve it.

STEP ONE

Write down five reasons why you dislike exercise: e.g. Because I'm no good at physical things.

How true are your reasons? For instance, what do you mean by 'no good at physical things'? Who told you this? Does it matter that you can't be 'good'? How can you challenge the above beliefs?

STEP TWO

Write down exactly what you want to change about your body. e.g. I want to be healthy and look better.

STEP THREE

Now write down why. e.g. Because I'm sick of feeling unfit and looking flabby.

Before you go on take a good look at that reason. If you've put because I want a boyfriend, because I want people to think I am beautiful, etc. you're on the wrong track. You need to change *your* attitude to yourself, not other people's. Making yourself fitter, more confident and more assertive might help get you a boyfriend but it won't directly lead to one.

STEP FOUR

Now list all the ways you can start changing right now, this instant. e.g. Climb stairs, go for a walk, learn to cycle.

If you're not sure how to change, then you may have to do some extra work here. Check out your local library or local sport centre to see what's available where you live, or go to your video shop for a home fitness video.

STEP FIVE

Now work out how you can actually make your plan work in everyday life.
e.g. I'll walk to school. I'll walk up stairs instead of taking the lift. I'll swim twice a week. I'll get my friends round for video exercise sessions.

Remember to set realistic goals or else you won't stick to them. Also use this last section to try and pinpoint your weak areas. For instance, if you want to eat

healthily but
find you give in
every time you go
to the doughnut shop,
then only go there once a
month, instead of once a
week. If you hate swimming when
it's cold, find something else to do in
the winter months e.g. walking (never go alone)
and/or home aerobics (you'll have no excuse not to
get to class!).

STEP SIX

Lastly, WORK TO YOUR OWN PLAN. For instance, if
you choose to lose weight by exercising, don't listen
to people who tell you how you should do it (unless
they happen to be a fitness expert). Choose your own
goal and work towards it at your own pace. This stops
unwanted advice, feelings of failure and peer pressure.
There's nothing worse than having made a decision to
change something in your life than to have everyone
tell you what to do.

The fact is you can get fit and healthy right now, this second. All you have to do is make a decision that this is what YOU want to do, for YOURSELF.

20 tips for getting active

1   If you're totally inactive and want to get fit, start by doing something you can easily fit into your life, like walking. Walking is not only good for all your muscles but also increases your cardiovascular strength – it's good all-round exercise. American studies have shown that walking a mile a day reduces the risk of osteoporosis in later life.

2   Try roller-skating for aerobic fitness, strength and flexibility.

3   Dancing is fun, good for your muscles and your cardiovascular strength (and you can do it alone in your bedroom).

4   Climbing the stairs when you're out shopping is better than taking the escalator.

5   If you are interested in a particular sport and don't know how to get involved contact: The Sports Council 0171 388 1277.

6   Time whatever exercise you do. To stay in shape, the Sports Council recommend 20 minutes of moderate exercise, three times a week.

7   Do everything twice. The extra energy used in repeating things like walking up and down the stairs will firm you up twice as quick.

8   If you feel embarrassed about exercising in public, either rent a fitness video or buy one of the many fitness magazine for exercises you can do in your bedroom.

9 Remember, every little bit helps. Getting up to switch the TV over, walking to school, even wandering round the shops.

10 Set yourself realistic goals – aiming to run the marathon may be a bit over the top.

11 Make exercise something fun and part of your everyday life, not something you have to fit into your schedule.

12 Think about activities you and your friends could do together, like swimming.

13 Don't force yourself to take up something you know you hate.

14 Ask your PE teacher or a fitness instructor at your local Leisure Centre for help in setting up an exercise plan that works for you.

15 Try a sport you may have written off as being too hard for you. Learning to participate in a sport is 50% confidence and 50% effort.

16 Remember, you don't have to excel at the exercise you choose to do.

17 Try and get your family involved in becoming active. This will not only give you moral support but get them fit too.

18 Don't tell everyone what you're up to unless you want people giving you their opinions all the time.

19 Be aware that you can incorporate exercise into everything you do, including watching TV – you could lie on the floor and do sit ups or stretches.

20 Check your local leisure centre out. It might be cheaper to join than you think.

Where to go for help

If you need further information or advice about the issues covered in this book, contact one of the organisations listed below.

Eating Disorders Association
Sackville Place
44–48 Magdalen Street
Norwich
Norfolk
NR3 1JE
Tel: helpline 01603 621414
Youthline 01603 765050

Overeaters Anonymous
Tel: 01426 984674

The Sports Council
Tel: 020 273 1500

Health Education Authority
Trevelyan House
30 Great Peter Street
London
SW1P 2HW
Tel: 020 7222 5300

The Health Education Authority (HEA) publish leaflets and books on a range of health topics, which are usually available at a local health promotion clinic (check in the phone book for your nearest clinic).

Childline
Tel: 0800 1111

This is a free and confidential telephone helpline for any young person in trouble or danger.

Glossary

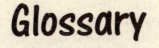

ANOREXIA
An eating disorder characterised by a fear of becoming fat and a refusal of food, leading to illness and sometimes death.

BULIMIA
An eating disorder leading to anxiety about putting on weight. This leads to compulsive overeating followed by vomiting.

CALORIES
The energy value of food. Used as a unit of measurement to show how much food, will produce how much energy.

COMFORT EATING
Eating not because you're hungry but because you believe it will help you to feel better.

COMPULSIVE EATING
The impulse to eat when not physically hungry.

DIET
A low food regimen whereby you limit the amount of food you eat.

DIURETIC
Medication that increases the flow of urine.

EATING DISORDER
The collective name given to people who have disturbed eating patterns.

FAT
A naturally occurring substance which is essential to the human body to coat our body's cells and supply our body with the energy and fuel it needs to do everyday things.

HORMONES
Brain chemicals released by glands which activate certain body functions such as the growth of the sex hormones and the menstrual cycle.

LAXATIVES
Medication that loosens the bowels.

METABOLISM
The rate at which your body utilises energy (and burns up the food you've eaten).

OBESITY
A medical definition to state a person is excessively overweight.

OVERWEIGHT
Over the 'normal' weight range for your height and age.

Index

Another essential Wise Guide

DRUGS

Anita Naik

What are drugs?
What do they do to your mind -
and your body?
Are you under pressure to take drugs?
Do you have friends who already do?
What are the risks - and how should
you deal with them?

Alcohol and amphetamines, tobacco and
cannabis, solvents and steroids - know
the realities and explode the myths with
this essential wise guide.

Another essential Wise Guide

PERIODS

Charlotte Owen

Everyone worries about getting their
first period.
What does it mean?
When will it happen?
How will it feel?
Will everyone else know?
And what on earth do you do?

This essential book explains all you'll
ever need to know about one of the most
important times in your life!

Another essential Wise Guide

BULLYING

Michele Elliott

Nearly everyone is bullied at some point in their life. But what exactly does bullying mean? Are there practical things you can do to stop it? How do you deal with your anger and frustration? How can you learn to make friends and respect yourself? If you're a bully, can you ever change your behaviour?

Don't suffer in silence. Learn how to beat the bullies and restore your self-esteem with this essential wise guide.

ORDER FORM
Wise Guides

0 340 75297 1	DIVORCE & SEPARATION	£3.99
0 340 75299 8	SELF-ESTEEM	£3.99
0 340 63604 1	PERIODS	£3.99
0 340 69973 6	DRUGS	£3.99
0 340 71483 2	BULLYING	£3.99
0 340 71042 X	SEX	£3.99
0 340 74419 7	YOUR RIGHTS	£3.99

All Hodder Children's books are available at your local bookshop or newsagent, or can be ordered direct from the publisher. Just tick the titles you want and fill in the form below. Prices and availability subject to change without notice.

Hodder Children's Books, Cash Sales Department, Bookpoint, 39 Milton Park, Abingdon, Oxon, OX14 4TD, UK. If you have a credit card you may order by telephone – (01235) 400414.

Please enclose a cheque or postal order made payable to Bookpoint Ltd to the value of the cover price and allow the following for postage and packing:

UK & BFPO – £1.00 for the first book, 50p for the second book, and 30p for each additional book ordered, up to a maximum charge of £3.00.
OVERSEAS & EIRE – £2.00 for the first book, £1.00 for the second book, and 50p for each additional book.

Name ....

Address ....

....

....

If you would prefer to pay by credit card, please complete the following:
Please debit my Visa/Access/Diner's Card/American Express (delete as applicable) card no:

----- ----- ----- ----- ----- ----- ----- ----- ----- ----- ----- ----- ----- ----- ----- -----

Signature ....

Expiry Date ....